SIMON
KENTON

D1287550

SIMON KENTON

Library of Congress Cataloging-in-Publication Data

Clark, Thomas Dionysius, 1903-
    Simon Kenton, Kentucky scout / by Thomas D. Clark ; illustrated by
Edward Shenton; edited and introduction by Melba Porter Hay.
        p.   cm.
    Originally published: New York : Farrar & Rinehart, 1943.
    Includes bibliographical references.
    ISBN 0-945084-38-2 : $17.95. -- ISBN 0-945084-39-0 : $8.95
        1. Kenton, Simon, 1755-1836. 2. Scouts and scouting--Northwest,
Old--Biography. 3. Scouts and scouting--Kentucky--Biography.
4. Frontier and pioneer life--Northwest, Old 5. Frontier and
pioneer life--Kentucky. 6. Northwest, Old--History--1775-1865.
7. Kentucky--History--To 1792. I. Shenton, Edward, 1895-   .
II. Hay, Melba Porter, 1949-   . III. Title.
F517.K383C53 1993
976.9'02'092--dc20
[B]   93-20718
                                                                CIP
                                                                 AC

Published by:
The Jesse Stuart Foundation
P.O. Box 391
Ashland, KY 41144
1993

SIMON KENTON

KENTUCKY SCOUT
by
THOMAS D. CLARK

Illustrated by
Edward Shenton

Edited and with an Introduction
by
Melba Porter Hay

The Jesse Stuart Foundation
Ashland, Kentucky
1993

DEDICATED TO
THE KENTUCKY HISTORICAL
SOCIETY

CONTENTS

INTRODUCTION

Adventure story, biography, western, history, *Simon Kenton, Kentucky Scout* fits all these descriptions. Its vivid, intense language tells the story of Kentucky's exploration and settlement through the life of the young Indian scout. Time after time Kenton saved early pioneers and kept them from being forced to return to the eastern side of the mountains. It was largely because of the activities of men such as Simon Kenton and Daniel Boone that Americans, who had taken over a century and a half to reach the Appalachian Mountains, were able to complete their expansion across the entire continent within the next seventy-five years.

Just as the name Simon Kenton immediately calls to mind images of Kentucky's early frontier, the name Thomas D. Clark is instantly identified with Kentucky history. Since winning a scholarship in 1928 to do graduate work at the University of Kentucky, the Mississippi native has published more about the Commonwealth's history and done more to preserve its documentary heritage than any other person. Not only has he written numerous books and articles about Kentucky, the frontier, and the South, he has given untold numbers of talks across the Commonwealth.

No other historian in the state has achieved name recognition or popularity to match Tom Clark's. His years of distinguished service include thirty-seven years on the faculty at the University of Kentucky, twenty-five of which he served as history department chairman, and stints during his retirement at the University of Louisville and Eastern Kentucky University, as well as Indiana University. Indeed, the word "retirement" must be used cautiously when referring to Clark's work during the more than quarter century since he left the University of Kentucky. His schedule of speaking, researching, writing, and serving on committees and boards that seek to preserve and promote the state's history would exhaust a person half his age.

Although Clark has made many notable contributions to Kentucky, perhaps none has been more significant and lasting than his vision for preserving the sources from which history is written. That vision led to the development of the Special Collections Department at the University of Kentucky's Margaret I. King Library, the founding of the University Press of Kentucky, the establishment of the Kentucky Department for Libraries and Archives, and the creation of the Oral History Commission. He has been a supporter of the Kentucky Historical Society as well as numerous other local, state, and national historical organizations.

His keen analyses of Kentucky's political, economic, and educational problems have proved correct time after time. For decades he has urged the state to adopt a new, workable constitution. Many portions of the 1990 Kentucky Education Reform Act were changes he had long advocated.

Clark's untiring work has earned him many honors and awards. He has received numerous honarary degrees, a Guggenheim fellowship (1964-65), and in 1990 the Kentucky General Assembly named him Historian Laureate of Kentucky for life, declaring that he is "like our bountiful land, lakes,

mountains and streams . . . a unique Kentucky resource deserving
of the highest honor." He has also served as editor of the *Journal
of Southern History* and president of both the Southern Historical
Association and the Organization of American Historians.

When I started graduate school at the University of Kentucky
in 1971, Tom Clark's name was already a legend in the history
department. By then he was well established in his retirement
career, but his presence was still strongly felt on campus and
stories about him abounded. Later, when I started work for *The
Papers of Henry Clay* documentary editing project, I found that
it was a program initiated by Clark. During my eleven years
with the Clay Papers, I had occasion to call on him many times
to clarify some point about the project's history. He was always
willing to help with courtesy and a sense of humor, which
prompted him to refer to me as "Mrs. Clay." Just as he had been
present at the creation of the Clay Papers, he was there to take
part in the conclusion celebration when the project was completed
in June 1991 after forty years. Without his support, it would
never have been undertaken and certainly could never have been
finished. In the early days he even purchased Henry Clay letters
so they would be available for the project to include in its
volumes. (This proved to be a shrewd investment as Clay letters
have appreciated greatly in value.)

When I started work at the Kentucky Historical Society in
1991 after the Clay project was completed, I found Dr. Clark
on the Society's Executive Committee. He is a strong supporter
of the Society's mission of collecting, preserving, and dis-
seminating information about the Commonwealth's history.
He is also one of the most vocal advocates of the proposal, now
in the planning stages, for the state to build a Kentucky History
Center to house the Society's offices, library, and museum.

A few years ahead of me in graduate school, my husband
had the opportunity I missed of studying under this Kentucky

legend. It made a lasting impression. He absorbed from Clark the idea that the history profession has a duty to take history to the people, not just to other historians, and that local history is important and should not be ignored.

The biography of Simon Kenton is an example of Clark's versatility and his desire to reach a variety of audiences. He wrote this work, which was first published in 1943, for a junior high school audience. While the biography's sentence structure and vocabulary are simple enough for young readers, it will appeal to a general audience as well. The brisk pace of the story, the vivid, lyrical descriptions of the early Kentucky landscape, interwoven with explanations of frontier culture and history, can inform, educate, and entertain anyone.

Of all the forms of history, biography is probably the most popular and one of the most difficult to do well. The writer must capture the subject's personality as well as the spirit of the time and place, providing enough background information about supporting characters and events to make it understandable without losing the subject in the narrative. As David McCullough, the prize-winning biographer of Harry Truman stated in a 1990 address at the National Archives, "Writing history and biography . . . is an art form. It should be, and it ought to be approached with all the same respect and all of the same aspirations that one would approach writing drama and fiction." He added that "it takes a great deal of imagination to write nonfiction," because the writer should be able to make the reader feel a part of the past. Few biographies succeed in this task, but certainly *Simon Kenton* does.

The action-packed story takes Kenton from his birth in 1755 in Fauquier County, Virginia, to 1784-85, when he established his own station in present-day Mason County. His flight from home at age sixteen when he believed he had killed William Leachman, his attempts to find the fabled caneland of Kentucky, his courageous rescue of Daniel Boone during an Indian attack at Boonesbourgh, and his friendships with such colorful, diverse, and controversial characters as George Rogers Clark, Simon Girty, and Chief John Logan are surpassed in drama only by his daring theft of the Indians' horses at Chillicothe and his subsequent capture and eventual escape. While he was held captive, Kenton showed an almost superhuman stamina as he endured a Mazeppa ride, ran the dreaded gantlet several times, and withstood beatings, broken bones, and other tortures. In retrospect, it seems only the hand of Providence could have provided the timely intervention of Simon Girty and John Logan which postponed his execution. Even more extraordinary was the sudden rainstorm which drenched the fire when the flames were already shooting up to consume Simon, who was tied to the stake. The appearance of a French Canadian trader almost immediately thereafter, his success in persuading the Indians to allow the prisoner to be taken to the British for interrogation, and Kenton's ability simply to walk away from Detroit and return to Kentucky are equally amazing.

Although this is a story told primarily from the point of view of the white man, Clark makes clear on many occasions that Kentucky's settlement was purchased at the price of great pain and suffering for both whites and Native Americans. He notes that "failure to regard the Indian as a human being often led to some horrible atrocities on the part of the white frontiersman." He describes the massacre of Mingo Chief John Logan's family by Daniel Greathouse and his "murderous band" and the destruction of Indian villages and crops as the two conflicting cultures struggled for survival.

When this work closes, Simon Kenton at age thirty is attempting to adjust to a Kentucky that is being rapidly populated. The Native Americans have been defeated and pushed farther west, and there is no longer any need for an Indian scout.

Simon has established his own settlement in northern Kentucky and gathered his family about him. The most dangerous, exciting portion of his life was finished. But, the reader may wonder at the close of this work, what about Kenton's remaining fifty-one years? How would he adjust to a more structured and sophisticated society?

Simon Kenton had already shown his dislike of farm work and his disdain for a fixed routine. His restless spirit, as well as his careless attitude toward financial and legal matters, resembled those of his friend, Daniel Boone. For a few years he succeeded in having a quiet and relatively prosperous life. In 1787 he married Martha Dowden, and the couple had four children. He acquired large tracts of land, ran a store in the little town of Washington in present-day Mason County, and built his family a new brick house. Then, tragedy struck. The house burned, killing his wife, who was pregnant with their fifth child. A little over a year later, in 1798, he married Martha's cousin, Elizabeth Jarboe, and they had five children.

At the end of 1798 Kenton moved his family to Ohio, where he spent the remainder of his life in poverty, moving several times. Defective land titles cost him much of his land. He made four trips to Missouri, visited Daniel Boone, and considered moving there. On a trip to Washington, Kentucky, in 1820 he was arrested for debt. Although there was a public outcry against his imprisonment, he remained in jail until December 1821, when the Kentucky legislature repealed the debtor's law.

Kenton returned to his home near Zanesville, Ohio, where he died on April 29, 1836. He was buried there, but in 1865 his remains were moved to Urbana. In 1840 the Kentucky legislature named a new county in northern Kentucky in his honor, and in 1884 the state of Ohio erected a monument to him in Urbana.

Certainly, few characters in the annals of Kentucky history have been more colorful or more important to its early survival.

Through *Simon Kenton,* Tom Clark has captured the feeling of the time, the place, and the personality. Readers of all ages will thrill to this exciting story of life on the Kentucky frontier.

Melba Porter Hay
Kentucky Historical Society
March 1993

CHAPTER 1

A Virginia Spring

Mark Kenton rubbed his calloused hands together and drawled, "Well, hit's hyar at last, Jim! Spring's shore been a spell a-comin' this year."

"Tiny" Jim Martin nodded agreement. The storekeeper knew how badly his neighbors wanted spring to come. Half to himself he said, "Folks around hyar been complainin' mightily about having nothing to eat but salt meat and corn bread. They ar' a-wantin' to get their gardens and fields planted."

The fields and woods were gray from a heavy rainstorm and large fleecy clouds drifted close down over the sharp-pointed tops of the Virginia mountain pines. Occasionally the huge blue belly of one of the clouds playfully flipped upside down and shone brightly in the little puddles of sunlight. A large sunny spot rolled wildly across the brown pasture. As the ball of sunlight passed out of sight there was a shrill call from a cocky redbird.

The redbird and clouds were sure signs of spring. Mark pulled his lean body up from the clumsy stool and stretched his arms high over his head. He was going, he told Jim Martin, to get ready to plant another crop on Richard Graham's place. It was time to begin work. He had seen maple and dogwood buds swelling; oak and chestnut branches were putting out tiny dogeared shoots.

Mark threw a sack of goods over his right shoulder and stumbled toward the door. Before going out he rested one huge, bony hand on the overhead door facing and turned to look at the little storekeeper. "I've already got six children, and thar's a seventh 'un a-comin soon."

The weather-beaten farmer's way home was up a long ridge. As his feet bumped carelessly against the loose stones in the path, Mark began to think of the long struggle he faced to make his family a living that year. Everything one did in the Virginia piedmont country was difficult. Running through his mind was the haunting story of his hard life on stingy old Dick Graham's red-clay acres.

Years ago he had built a cabin on his rented land underneath the wide, blue rim of Bull Run Mountain. It was built by what the pioneers called "main strength and awkwardness." Neighbors had helped him drag the long hewn-pine logs from their rocky beds on the hillside. They were then notched and carefully stacked into the four crude walls of a one-room cabin. The side walls were built high above the ceiling runner to allow room for a deep loft. Long, slender skinned poles were pegged into gawky "a-frames" to receive the lathes on which clapboards were to be weighted with heavy stones and split-log binders. On one side a wide door was cut through the wall, after a riven-board facing had been pegged firmly to the logs to hold them in place. On the other side a small window was cut, so that the sun in its course could shine in at the window in the morning and through the door in the afternoon. At the south end was a rock-and-stick chimney with a yawning mouth which would receive long lengths of green logs. A gooseneck back created a draft which drew off the smoke but forced the heat into the room.

Inside was a well-matched puncheon floor which a skilled neighbor had hewn flat with a foot adz. A crude table, made from half a split log with four spraddling pole legs wedged into large auger holes, stood in one corner. Three or four stools made from flat sawed bolts of a tree trunk served as chairs. In each of the back corners were crude handmade beds, and overhead along the blank walls were long hickory pegs on which to hang clothing. In one corner a peg ladder went up to a trap door in the ceiling. One touch more and the cabin was in readiness for living. Over the door was a pair of neatly polished buckhorns to hold the family rifle.

This was Mark Kenton's new home—a large room downstairs, and space for a bedroom in the loft. He had built it on the ground from such strong materials as nature supplied him. It was by no means a comfortable house, but it kept out most of the wind and rain. Varmints could not molest its inhabitants, and it would stand off a moderate Indian attack. Its huge fireplace, piled high with blazing hardwood logs, supplied enough heat to burn a man to a crisp on one side while the cold air came through the cracks in the wall and froze him on the other. Cherry-red coals drawn from underneath the bottom logs were hot enough to cook the family meal. This was the home to which proud young Mark Kenton fetched his happy young bride, Mary Miller Kenton, eighteen years before, and here his six children had been born. Now there was to be another.

CHAPTER 2

Seventh Child

The weather grew milder, and by April Mark Kenton and the older children were making ready to break the rough red ground to plant corn for bread and tobacco, for taxes and rent. In the first week of April, Mary gave birth to another son. He was a sturdy little fellow with strong muscles, a large round face, and light yellow hair. He gave every indication of being as rugged as the huge chestnut trees which sent up their branches to tower high above their neighbors along the rim of the hill which hemmed in the little cabin.

A seventh child was no ordinary one. Old frontier granny women in Virginia had long before said that seventh children, especially boys, were born with talents which no other child had. They had special powers to cure disease. They could accomplish things in life which other children could not.

It was with great satisfaction and pride that clumsy Mark Kenton took his sturdy new son in his arms. The birth of a son to a man was no ordinary happening, and boys were the greatest assets to the frontier country. And children could be mighty entertaining in a home. Later on they could relieve an old man crippled by rheumatism from hard work in the field. Mark Kenton looked forward to the day when he could let up from his hard labors in the rocky cornfield and sit on a stump and watch his children labor in his place.

These fine sons of Mark's would play a noble part in breaking the way to a new civilization in the wilderness. They would make the name of Kenton both dignified and numerous. This new son should have a good Biblical name like his brothers Mark and John and like his father. He should be called Simon.

As the spring months passed, there was much talk along the Virginia piedmont frontier of the approaching war between the British and the French and Indians. George Washington, from the nearby Potomac River valley, had just come back from a diplomatic visit to the western woods with wily Christopher Gist as a guide. He had come home to notify his people that he had failed in his mission. War was inevitable. Mark Kenton's neighbors were vitally interested in this approaching border struggle. Their homes were threatened. They sat for long hours before their gaping wide-mouthed fireplaces and discussed frontier affairs.

Old Man Leachman came at night to sit and talk with the Kentons. "I'll tell you, Mark, we're in for trouble," said the wrinkled old settler. "Them Frenchmen don't want this country settled by the likes of us. Them and the Indians want to hang to the woods for the varmints. They will drive us back if they can."

Mark was disturbed. "Hit's going to be a mighty tough fight," said he. "Every man in this country is going to have to fight 'em back with rifle and ax. Our women and children will be in danger." Mark spat into the fire and was silent for a moment. He was running over in his mind the horrors of frontier warfare. "When them French and Indian robbers come, they'll tomahawk everybody," he said.

The Kenton boys, Mark and John, listened intently to the war talk and shuddered at the horrible thought of having to fight the Indians.

Mary Kenton sat by in silence with her daughters and listened to the conversation. She hoped the French and Indian raiders would be kept away from her children. She ran her protecting hand along the back of the newborn child and prayed that he would be spared from savage attacks in which young babies were destroyed while their screaming mothers looked on.

Across the river in Maryland General Edward Braddock, a haughty English army officer, was bustling around getting his army organized. General Braddock was wholly unfamiliar with American geography, and he was far too proud to listen to the advice of so ordinary a soldier as George Washington or any of his buckskinned followers who knew the western woods. He was going to the head of the Ohio River to fight a European open-field war in the thick woods of that region. English soldiers were to march in closed ranks, clothed in their bright red coats, crisscrossed with broad white straps. Such an army was a grand sight in England, but it was a poor fighting force in America.

Old-timers of the backwoods looked at the grand army cutting Braddock's road from Cumberland, Maryland, toward Fort Duquesne and shook their heads. They knew about the fighting tactics of the French and their Indians allies. Long, bony arms reached above cabin doors to take down slim-barreled flintlock rifles from their buckhorn rests. Flints were picked, tubes were oiled, and ramrods with their tow swabs were thrust through barrels. The men of the Bull Run Mountain frontier were going away to fight a war with the young surveyor-soldier George Washington as their commander. They were a wild-looking crew of ragamuffins as compared with the neat crossbelted and redcoated soldiers of General Braddock. No two rifles were alike. Their clothes were made of coarse deerskin and linsey-woolsey hunting shirts whose baggy skirts hung below their knees. Loose, bulging trousers were gathered into leggings, which connected with homemade moccasins. There were broad-brimmed, low-crowned beaver hats, whose brims flopped down over the face, and skin caps that held back long, greasy locks of hair. Slung over every shoulder was a bulging bullet pouch, a sharp-pointed powder horn, and a roomy provision sack.

Beside Braddock's fine troops, Mark Kenton's spunky neighbors presented a shabby picture. They were going to war to win; dress parade and manual of arms meant nothing to them. There was an even greater difference underneath their coarse clothes. These Virginia riflemen were going voluntarily to defend their homes. They knew nothing of fighting in closed ranks, nor did they pay too much attention to orders given by their officers. They carried their own supplies and picked their own points from which to fight. Ammunition was scarce, and they knew the value of accurate shooting. It was they who had given real meaning to the old frontier cry of "every man to his own tree."

One look at this ragtag-and-bobtail army was enough for the swaggering Braddock. He believed these men could not fight, and he was certain they would not obey his command. He went his own stubborn way, refusing to listen to the advice of seasoned frontiersmen. When he was surprised by the enemy near Fort Duquesne, his fine army was put to hopeless rout, and the general himself was killed. Washington's men were disgusted at the blundering tactics used by the British officers, but they retreated with their leader and formed a new line at Fort Necessity.

This all happened the year Simon Kenton was born. After Braddock's defeat, the conversations around the pioneers' firesides grew more excited. The fight had come closer home. Braddock's ridiculous blunder had exposed the frontier homes of the great Virginia piedmont pioneers to Indian attacks. Mary Kenton sat and listened to this frightening talk. She drew the covers tighter around her sleeping baby and prayed for his safety.

From the time he could understand the meaning of a half dozen words, Simon Kenton was hearing of Indians and border wars. All this talk appealed to his childish imagination. Indians impressed him as being interesting people. He sprawled upon his stomach before his father's big fire and listened intently to tales of the frontier told by his brothers and sisters. Where other less ventursome children have been lulled by countless repetitions of the fantastic Mother Goose tales, Simon dropped off to sleep to dream of bloody fights with Indians and of successful hunting ventures.

His young mind was being deeply impressed by these tales of wonder, and quietly he was making a firm resolution to see for himself these things in the great woods when he grew up. Every ridge, every branch, creek, and river and tree was part of a great natural mystery. Rough bark on the north side of a tree or the broken branch of a bush was a lesson in reading. The swift current of a tiny stream bustling off to make connections with a larger one was an elementary lesson in mathematics. Tracks of an animal impressed delicately in fresh mud, stray hairs sticking to the frayed end of a hollow log, the drifting down of a bird's feather were real lessons in biology. From the very beginning of Simon Kenton's life those were his textbooks.

Simon's young neighbors in backwoods Virginia were put to work almost at the moment they started walking. They could bring armloads of wood from the woodpile and buckets of water from the spring. The three older Kenton boys, and even the girls, had gone through an apprenticeship from doing the simple tasks about the farm to that of performing more difficult ones. Always the farm was a busy place.

Every season brought its special tasks. Each spring there were stubborn sprouts which had to be cut from around the many stumps which dotted Richard Graham's hillside fields. Bodies of fallen trees, which had been deadened years before, had to be chopped into short lengths, rolled into piles, and burned.

The wind was forever blowing down the crazy zigzag fences, or rails rotted and had to be replaced. Weeds and tall grass grew rapidly toward maturity in the fall, and their dead stalks remained through the winter to clutter garden patches when planting time came. Before truck patches could be planted, all this coarse rubbish had to be raked and burned so that smooth seedbeds could be prepared for the tender garden plants. Everybody had a job in preparing for a new crop.

When buds swelled under the warming influence of the lengthening spring days, Mark Kenton brushed the long winter hair from the coats of his skinny horses and got ready for plowing. When he was first married, he broke his land with a hand mattock, but as children began to appear, he could no longer break land enough in this way to produce a living. During the winter the elder Kenton had spent long hours weaving tightly twisted rolls of coarse corn shucks into collars for the horses. He had cut strong thick traces, bridles, and backbands from green cowhides and had fashioned rough plow beams and handles with his broadax and drawing knife. Iron plows were unknown, and Mark Kenton fashioned wooden wings and points to his plowfoot. The points he tipped with iron so the plow could be forced into the tight, rocky soil.

The horses were hitched one ahead of the other. A girl or a younger boy led them along the row while Mark and the older boys wrestled with the plow. As a man held fast to the handles and guided it along the furrow, the others forced the beam to bite into the ground. Rocks and stumps tossed the plowmen back and forth as though they were sailors on a stormy sea.

When the ground was broken, and the mellow soil heaped into narrow, peaked rows, it was ready for planting. The girls went ahead with splint baskets looped over their arms, dropping grains of corn at regular intervals, while their father and brothers followed on horse-drawn drags and covered it. Tiny tobacco seeds had already been sowed broadcast in long beds stretched across the sunny slope of a hillside.

When the long days of spring came, and the bold, round moon hung full and low on the short nights, the tobacco plants crowded their two large leaves and a tender bud high on slender stalks ready for transplanting. These plants were plucked one by one from the rich humus bed and dropped carefully a short step apart in the rows of the field. Each plant had to be thrust into the soft crown of the furrow and the soil packed down firmly with two rigid knuckles. Setting tobacco was hard work. Hour after hour the setters stooped over the soft rows with their backs in unnatural positions. Knuckles and forefingers grew raw from the constant hole digging and pressing of soil around the young tobacco roots.

When plants were growing in the fields, there were the eternal tasks of hoeing and plowing. It was a race between the farmer and a vigorous carpet of weeds to see who should claim the crop. Long spring and summer days kept Mark Kenton and his children busy. Even Mary Kenton would rush with her housework and take a turn at hoeing beside her husband. Mark was first with the hoe. It was said that he could clean the grass from an acre of corn a day. This was exhausting work. At night hoe and plow hands stretched their aching bodies on their hard beds and sank into a sleep as sound as death itself.

In the hot days of summer the tobacco grew rapidly, and then it ripened ready for the harvest. Every member of the family was called out to pluck the rapidly yellowing leaves from the stalks and then to pack them off to the curing barn, where they were spread on sticks to be smoked to a rich mellow brown over a smoldering fire.

After the leaves were cured, they were packed down in

hogsheads holding eight and nine hundred pounds each. A spindle ran through the middle of the barrel, and shafts were attached to the ends so it could be pulled in the form of a roller by a horse.

Each year Mark Kenton and his sons took the two-day trip down to Dumfries to sell their tobacco and to pay their landlord his rent and the crown its taxes. At night they camped with other "rollers." This was a social affair at which the men passed on news, spun yarns, and fought to their hearts' content. Here was one piece of work Simon enjoyed. He loved to sit by the annual "rolling" campfires and to hear the men tell their stories. Many of them were about the great woods. Occasionally an old timer would ease up to the fire and tell of his exciting experiences and narrow escapes in the French and Indian War. Or a hardy neighbor would repeat horror stories of Indian attacks upon the frontier cabins in which women and children were captured.

Frontiersmen enjoyed common workings. It was much more pleasant to make a holiday frolic of a mean job than to attempt to do it alone. Hardly had the tobacco crop been gathered before the corn was ready. The stalks were cut and dragged into piles for shocking. Ears were plucked and the fodder was stacked in the loft of the pole crib as feed for the cows and horses during the barren winter months. The corn was hauled to the crib and stacked to await the husking bee. Corn husking was a party affair at which the owner of the corn supplied food and music for a dance. Boys and girls chose partners and worked furiously to see who could win the prize for husking the most corn. The boy who found a red ear was given the privilege of kissing any girl he chose. It was all good fun, and a neighbor was obliged by having his corn shucked. Then came the dinner, and afterwards the fiddler urged on the rollicking square dance with his lively tunes until the sun came up.

Simon went to these parties when he was very young. It was great fun for him to stand by and see the older boys and girls husk the corn. He enjoyed the joking and laughing that went on around him. His brothers joined in the work and flirted with the girls.

William Leachman, a gangling neighbor boy, had a quick wit. He boasted, "I'm goin' to shuck a whole basketful of red ears tonight, and I'm goin' to kiss ever' girl hyar."

From the far corner of the pile of corn, brother Mark chuckled, "When I'm grown I'm not goin' t'plant nothin' but red-eared corn and then I can kiss ever' girl I want to."

Hardly had the boastful huskers ceased their banter before one of the boys stripped the shuck back from a long crimson ear with slender rows of shining grains. The girls gathered in a huddle and began to squeal and threaten to run away. Young Simon's blue eyes sparkled in glee. One of the girls had to give up a kiss as a reward for the red ear.

Simon's gay nature found great satisfaction in the party festivities and games of his neighbors. He was always ready for a frolic.

As Simon grew older he found the numerous workings more and more to his liking. Warm summer days matured the beans which had been planted in the cornfield. Always there were more beans than could be eaten at the time. The surplus crop was strung on long threads and dried in the sun for winter use. Just as in the husking of corn, neighbor boys and girls were invited to bean stringings and play parties.

For Simon the "stringin's" were happy occasions. The girls came with large needles and heavy thread, and the boys were present to help with the work. As soon as the couples were paired off, a race was begun to see which girl could make the longest string of beans in the shortest time. Simon stumbled in and out among the racing couples listening to the jokes and the laughter. Sometimes he took part in the teasing, and occasionally he took a liking for a couple and attempted to help it win the race.

When the beans had been strung, and the leaves began to pitch down from the apple trees, news was passed around that there was to be an apple-cutting party. Boys and girls cut apples in quarters and packed them down in earthenware crocks to be preserved with sulphur.

After the harvest season was over, Simon's mother got out her scrap bags. The quilting frames which had hung from the hooks in the ceiling were lowered on stout cords. In the kitchen there was much activity. Simon knew the signs. There was to be a quilting party and supper. Women and girls sewed bright patches on the quilt, and whipped down the edges with fancy stitches. The men and boys stood around the cabin door or sat by the fire and spun yarns of adventure.

When the last bright red patch had been whipped securely into place, the clumsy frame was again rolled up to the ceiling. The supper table was moved into its place. Mark Kenton had invited a good fiddler for the party, and as soon as the last mouthful of food was swallowed, Simon and his brothers cleared the cabin floor for the dance.

For lively young Simon, one season of the year followed another in quick succession. It was, for the Kentons and their neighbors, an endless process of life. The seasons changed too quickly for the Virginia frontiersmen ever to catch up with their work. Spring, summer, and fall for the Kentons were filled with planting and harvesting crops. Winter was a season of butchering and meat curing, cutting wood, making boards, hewing logs, and tanning leather. Never did Simon Kenton's people, struggling to make a living along Bull Run Creek, see the day when they felt they could leave off for a short time the hard struggle for existence.

CHAPTER 3

At Sixteen

For sixteen years Simon Kenton saw his family go through the same grinding yearly schedule of making a meager living from their poor Virginia hillside soil. The frontier way of life was hard if you worked at it, but Simon refused to work. His interest was in other things, if, as his parents often wondered, he had any interests at all. He abhorred the confinement of the cold log schoolroom where a heartless drunken Irish schoolmaster placed more emphasis upon failing boys for minor offenses than upon teaching them the more fundamental art of the three R's. There seemed to have been only one thing that Simon loved with passion, and that was the luxury of being idle. He would do little jobs around the place, but no one could get him to take hold of the plow or pick up an ax and go to the woods to split rails or cut wood all day. Even Mark could not prevail upon his son to follow his brothers' good example. Simon loved the woods and he absorbed a tremendous amount of knowledge of them. He never, however, loved hunting game just for the sake of hunting as did his young neighbors.

Thus it was that for sixteen years Simon Kenton was known as the laziest boy in the neighborhood. Every day for him was a struggle to keep out of the work and to steer clear of the confinement of the schoolroom. He learned a lot about the woods, but the most important lesson he learned was how to take care of himself and to stand an unreasonable amount of physical punishment.

Simon's fine body grew strong. His powerful muscular system rounded itself out. His legs grew stout; his fists became hard and round. They were fastened to arms whose muscles were as tough and flexible as small cabins. Heavy shoulders bulged under his linsey-woolsey shirt. Here was a rugged boy, said everybody who knew him, but "he was just plain no-account." The old granny women were right, after all. A seventh child was different, and Simon was certain proof of that fact. He was in the fairest way of becoming the biggest scapegrace in all the Virginia piedmont.

On the other hand, William, an older brother, was beginning to "amount to something." Richard Graham had employed him to watch over his scattered holdings in the Bull Run Mountain region. He had a horse, a saddle and bridle, and on Sundays he went to church meeting to "sidle up" to the girls. Aping the young Virginia squires who had Negro slaves to do their bidding, William commanded Simon to bridle and saddle his horse to fetch it to the house. The command was obeyed, but when William came down dressed in his best clothes and feeling important, Simon climbed into the saddle, whirled the horse about, and left his self-important brother afoot to make out as best he could. He might be gone for several days, and only after William made the most humble promises would he come home with the horse.

In Fauquier community a man's importance rested largely upon his ability to fight and to win at rough and tumble or to excel in other forms of physical prowess. Men met in neighborhood new grounds to roll logs into piles for burning. One

young bully challenged another to a test of strength with the stick. A strong young challenger offered to take the short end of a stick on the opposite side of a heavy green butt of a log and to "fasten" his opponent to the ground. From tugging at a handstick to fighting was a simple step. The man or boy who could hit hardest, gouge deepst, bite fiercest, or kick highest was the community bully. An independent man had to fight to assert himself. At the old field school he had to wield his fists both in antagonizing a neighbor and in self-defense. He fought with every physical aid at his command. Two bullies squared off at each other, and a circle of spectators drew up around them to take sides and to shout both encouragement and ridicule. They fought with their fists, butted hard with their heads, kicked, gouged at each other's eyes and stomachs, caught hold of mouthfuls of flesh, and bit with savage vengeance. They snatched out handfuls of hair and wrenched muscles until they gave way under the tormenting strain. This was rightly called "fist and skull" fighting.

Wherever men gathered on the frontier there were fights. Militia musters resulted in fist fights; at logrollings, square dances, around the campfires, on the tobacco "rollings," around the church doors, everywhere there were fights. Simon Kenton often stood by and shouted words of encouragement or derision at the fighters. Once in a while he himself was party to a fight, and he bit and clawed his way to victory or went home badly scratched and beaten.

Often between fights Simon sat on the top rail of his father's lot fence. He was flexing his right arm to see the knot of muscle pop up. Each time the firm arm muscle rose in a bulge, he puffed up with self-importance. "I'm sixteen years old," said Simon to himself. "Why, that's old enough to be a man in these parts. Sixteen years old and tough as a bull. I'm trouble on foot."

When the strutting Simon jumped down from the fence, he shouted, "Don't come near me. I'm real trouble."

Sixteen-year-old men with tough arm muscles in Fauquier County fell in love with a girl and married her. Simon now needed a wife. At all the neighboring cabins there were young girls. He decided to begin lookng around at the corn shuckings or at the church doors on Sundays.

Already Simon had stood around the cabin doors joking and bragging with the girls. But he hadn't "singled" out one. He wanted a wife who would make him a home. She had to be industrious to make up for his unwillingness to work. Plenty of girls were good listeners when Simon was showing off, but he was afraid they wouldn't do in a pinch.

Old Man Cummins had a good-looking girl named Ellen. Simon liked her looks, and she was a real hustler. She was seventeen and ready for marrying. She had long black hair, which hung down her back in two soft rolls. Her black eyes gave back exciting little reflections of light. Simon "marked out" Ellen for his sweetheart, but he was tongue-tied in her presence.

It was easy to joke and tease the other girls, but Ellen was different. She was easy for Simon to dream about, and when he was in a crowd of boys he could boast, "Boys, I'm goin' to court Ellen Cummins if it kills me!" But when he came face to face with her, he acted like a fool. A big lump rose in his throat, and he mumbled his words as though unable to talk.

At church one Sunday Simon wanted to ask Ellen to let him walk home with her, but all he could say as she passed him was "Howdy, Ellen." Before he could recover from his embarrassment, William Leachman had stepped up and beat his time.

Simon stood there in disgrace. His face had turned a shameful red. His hands grew heavy and gawky, and he could think of nothing more to say. But what hurt most of all, Ellen had treated him like a child, and she had gone off with William Leachman.

This was no way for a man to act. Simon knew he could never win the love of Ellen by being bashful. He would be positive in his courting and soon she would be his wife. But Simon was too slow. William Leachman was taking Ellen to square dances, the play parties, and to the occasional church meetings.

Everywhere Simon went, his neighbors were teasing him about letting Leachman take Ellen away from him. Even Mark and Mary smiled when they talked of their son's first falling in love. Maybe, after all, they hoped it would make Simon go to work. If he did not, he could never support a wife.

The boys laughed at Simon and chided him: "Why, Simon, are you going to let William Leachman hook you back from the lick log?" Or they infuriated him: "Simon, Ellen Cummins wants a man who'll hustle for a living. She can't take chances with a loafer like you." These taunts burned their way deeply into Simon's conscience.

Before long the very sight of the loose-jointed Leachman was maddening. Simon's Irish blood boiled in his veins and his heart thumped violently. His long fingers gouged savagely into the palms of his hands as his fists tightened into hard knots. One day soon he was going to fight his long-haired rival "rough and tumble."

Ellen Cummins knew what a frontier woman's life was, and she was afraid Simon could never make her a living. He was a rollicking, good-natured boy. But he was only a boy. William Leachman was older, and he worked hard. Everybody in the community talked of his industry and thrift. "He will make some girl a fine husband," they said. Ellen was quick to make up her mind that she was going to marry him.

Ellen's marriage to William Leachman was a grand frontier affair. For days before the wedding her whole family was busy making ready for the big party. Her father and brothers went hunting and fetched home two quarters of fine venison. They killed a yearling and a pig and prepared the meat for roasting over live coals in the fireplace. A turkey and several chickens were cooped up in the back yard awaiting their turn. Ellen and her mother gathered potatoes and vegetables. Big heads of cabbage were split in quarters and cooked tender with hunks of fresh pork. Potatoes were roasted in their skins. Huge sweet potato cobbler pies were baked, and pots of mush made ready. For days before the wedding neighbor women had brought in baskets of food, and they had helped to prepare the wedding dinner.

At last Ellen's wedding day arrived. It was a fine morning, and the wedding was to be at noon at the Leachman cabin. When the ceremony was over, the crowd would accompany the couple to the Cummins's home.

Soon after midmorning Ellen, mounted behind her father, set off by a back trail to William's home. The preacher and the guests were waiting for them. When she arrived, the girls helped to straighten out her heavy linsey dress and pushed her dainty wedding cap back from her forehead so that her beautiful oval face was outlined by a rim of black hair.

The big room of the cabin was crowded. There was a ring of women and girls in front, and behind them were the men and boys. The preacher stood with his back to the fireplace. William took Ellen's arm at the shed-room door and led her forward to stand before the preacher. The ceremony was short, and almost before she knew it, Ellen had become William Leachman's wife.

Hardly had the preacher finished his ceremony before the boys were leading their girls out to the horses and getting ready to go to the big dinner. William led his bride to his horse and lifted her to the cushion behind his saddle. It was a merry procession. On every side there were boys with girls mounted behind them. Young show-offs were wheeling their horses about and challenging other boys to race them. They teased the squealing girls and kept the whole party in an uproar.

When the procession was almost within sight of Ellen's house, two of the boys accepted the challenge to run for the bottle. Ellen's father held up a bottle of whisky and promised it to the winner at the end of a half-mile race. It was a hazardous ride. The woods were thick, vines hung low, and there were holes where tree stumps had rotted. But a good horseman could ride it without harm. It was a real accomplishment to win the bottle, and it made a good impression on the girls.

When the winner came riding back for the prize, there was a shout of congratulations. The bottle of whisky was handed over, and quickly it passed from mouth to mouth as a toast to the winner. All this was preliminary to the big dinner.

The whole morning Ellen's mother and a company of neighbor women had worked over the fireplace preparing the food. Before the wedding party arrived they loaded the table with venison, beef, pork, cabbage, potatoes, beans, peas, mush, and molasses. Old Man Cummins rushed on ahead after the race to bring in the big brown jug of whisky which he had hidden in the stable loft.

As the jug went around, the feasters grew merry. When the last mouthful of potato cobbler had been swallowed, the fiddler struck up the popular dance tune, "Barbara Allen." Standing on a log stool the caller ordered the couples around in quick order.

One after the other, the fiddler struck up new tunes. There were "Fisher's Horn Pipe" and then "Old Joe Clark," "Lord Elfin's Knight," "Leather Britches," and "Hog Drovers."

William Leachman led Ellen onto the floor for the opening set, but the bride and groom were not supposed to stay longer. When the opening set had been completed, they withdrew to the side lines to watch the dance. As they backed away the caller's shrill voice rose in loud command for the boys to:

Swing your partners and the one you meet,
That's what makes the swing so sweet.
Lady 'round the lady and the gents go slow.
Lady 'round gents and gents don't go.

Never was a couple happier. William was so proud of his beautiful bride that he could not take his eyes from her. He sat on the side of a bed with his arm about his wife when in walked Simon Kenton. Simon was an uninvited guest. He swaggered through the door in bold defiance of the social custom of his community. He had come to ruin the wedding party. Without ceremony he forced himself down between William Leachman and his young wife and undertook to take her away from him.

Simon acted foolishly. He gave William Leachman an excuse

to shoot him. Such a highhanded act on the frontier did not usually go unnoticed. To come between a man and his wife was a matter of life and death. But Simon was young and he was blinded by jealousy. A good whipping would be enough to bring him to his senses.

One of the Leachman boys asked Simon to come and have a drink, and when he was on the outside William threatened him with a whipping. Back and forth the two fought, Simon to salve his burning disappointment at losing his sweetheart and William to avenge injury to his dignity as a married man.

Simon was soundly thrashed. His youthful muscles were not strong enough to overcome the heavy attack of the older man. He staggered home with blood dripping from his nose and mouth. His eyes were swollen, and huge black splotches appeared where William Leachman's fist had bruised his flesh. His clothes were torn and his body had been pounded and scratched raw. He was defeated. Ellen Cummins had gone out of his life, but worst of all the proud, brash Simon had been completely humiliated in a fight of his own making. He was whipped before a jeering circle of neighbors.

CHAPTER 4

Revenge

Lying abed nursing a body too sore to move, Simon began to moralize on his defeat. The Leachman boys had treated him unfairly. They had fought him in their own yard, and he was certain they had taken unfair advantage of him otherwise. He bagan to plan a new attack. Foolish boy that he was, Simon believed that by some unusual performance he could reclaim Ellen. He was positive he could at least whip William Leachman.

The day would come, Simon said to himself, when he would have an opportunity to repay blow for blow. William Leachman's nose would run blood, and his mouth should be cut to pieces. Simon planned how he would kick him, tear off his clothes, scratch his skin into long stripes with his tense fingers, and pound both eyes black. Leachman would have to be caught off alone, but that time would come.

Simon got his chance when Mark Kenton sent him over to William Leachman's new house to borrow a saw. When Simon arrived at the house, William was carrying a bundle of clapboards up to his father on the roof. The saw Simon wished to borrow had been left at the board tree a short distance in the woods. William volunteerd to go with Simon to get it. The two walked off into the woods, William ahead and Simon following in his tracks. As they walked along, Simon's anger reached the boiling point as he stared at the weaving shoulders of his enemy. The time had come and here was the chance he prayed for. At last he and William Leachman were alone, and they would settle the score fairly.

At the board tree Simon challenged William to a fight. The young husband was reluctant, but when Simon charged him, he bacame angry. They fought with hardened fists. First one landed a heavy blow and then the other, but soon the weight and strength of Leachman began to tell against Simon. Simon clinched his overpowering opponent, but he tripped and fell. His shoulders were pinned hard and fast to the ground. Again William Leachman was pounding him unmercifully as he had done on his wedding day. Simon's chances of getting away without a sound thrashing were slim. The time had come for quick thinking and careful strategy. He had already proved to his own satisfaction that he could not whip Leachman with main body strength.

Leachman's long oily hair hung down his back in a loose queue. Close by was a low-spreading thornbush. If only the infuriated Leachman could be maneuvered to that spot and his hair entangled in the bush, then there was a chance for Simon to whip him. If Simon's body was notoriously lazy, his mind was alert. He could make quick decisions and move quickly to execute them. Grabbing hold of the seat of Leachman's pants with his mouth, he bit and shoved him nearer to the bush. With one catlike move, he grabbed Leachman's greasy queue and entangled it securely in the matted branches of the thornbush.

At last, William Leachman was at Simon's mercy. Standing over his rival's writhing body, all the bitterness of a defeated suitor flared up in his soul. Every one of the many blows Leachman had landed upon his sore body stung him into a rage.

Like a flash, the humiliation of his limping retreat from the wedding party goaded him. Now he would have satisfaction. He would repay two blows for one, and he could send haughty Leachman home to Ellen Cummins battered and limping. He would tear off his clothes. He would black his eyes and cut his mouth.

Simon's revenge was to be complete. He landed right- and left-handed blows on the helpless William. He kicked and scratched at will. Simon had become a ferocious animal in his storm of wrath. All human mercy and sanity had left him.

William Leachman rolled and twisted, but the strong pigtail held him captive to the wiry brush. In a moment all movement became impossible. He settled back into a state of uncon-sciousness. Blood trickled from his nose and mouth. His face grew livid. His hands fell limply to his side. Leachman gave every appearance of being dead.

Simon was frightened. In his insane anger he had killed his opponent. He had gone too far, and now he would suffer a horrible punishment.

As Simon stared at the "lifeless" body of his rival, all the awful stories of hangings which the men had told around the tobacco "rolling" campfires flashed into his mind to taunt him. Older men had said murderers were hanged quickly for their crimes on the frontier. Courthouses and jails were few, and the community could not afford to take a chance with a man who would commit murder. They had told how a heavy rope was tied around the culprit's neck while he stood on a horse, and then the horse was made to jump out from under him, and his neck was broken by the fall. Or a crude scaffolding was built, and the criminal's body was dropped through a yawning trap door.

Simon was panic-stricken. Not far away he could hear the elder Leachman laying boards on William and Ellen's house. In a few moments the father would grow anxious and come to see what had happened to his son. He would find him dead, with his hair entangled in the bush. Simon knew that he would be accused of the death. Soon men from the neighborhood would come to his father's house to arrest him. They would hang him—hang him before his neighbors—before all the people who had seen him whipped at the wedding party.

Hot flashes came over his body. His mind worked quickly. Instantly he thought of the great western woods. His bruised muscles trembled, his courage to go home failed. When the enraged men of the nearby cabins came looking for him, he would be on his way to the romantic land beyond the mountains. The saw fell from his shoulders on the trail at a point halfway to his father's house. Simon Kenton stepped aside into the protective cover of the woods. He would go to the distant Ohio Valley, and there he would bury his identity.

One of Simon's neighbors had looked at his neck once and said that when a boy had so many moles he would surely hang. As Simon picked his way among the low underbrush on that April morning when he began his flight, his coarse linsey shirt bound his nervous throat. He had suddenly remembered the telltale ring of moles, and he was afraid the prophecy would come true. In a short time a hue and cry would be raised on his trail. Men and boys would come with ropes to find him. He would be hunted and chased just as were the foxes in the lower Virginia thickets.

Never in Simon's life had he stopped to think what it would be like to be afraid of something. In a quick resolution he determined that if he was to be chased like an animal, he would adopt animal habits. He would hide until nightfall and then turn his steps southwestward. To go the most direct route toward the Ohio River was to invite more trouble. Someone along the main trail to the headwaters of the river would certainly recognize him and he would be arrested. He would travel through the dense woods away from the centers of settlement with only his inborn sense of direction to guide him.

When he dressed that morning, he had pulled on his coarse linsey-woolsey trousers and the loose-fitting linsey shirt. He didn't even have a hat to cover his stubborn flaxen hair. A man had no use for a hat except when he was going somewhere or it was raining. He could even get along without a gun and a horse. Guns were needed only when one was hunting, and horses were useful for field work and an occasional trip to the water mill to have corn ground, or to pull hogsheads on the tobacco rollings.

All the equipment Simon had that morning was a shirt and a pair of trousers. He had nothing more but his courage, and that was badly shaken.

Noon came and the warm sun stood high overhead. The woods took on the stillness of that moment when time teetered between morning and afternoon. Nearby workmen of the community were going home to their dinner. All around were the shrill blasts of the dinner horns. Plowmen stripped their sweating beasts of their harnesses and led them to their stables to be watered and fed. Hoes were dropped where the first blast of the horn was heard, and the hoe hands walked lazily across the long brown stretches of freshly plowed ground. They were going home to eat hearty meals of hot corn bread, meat, and spring greens. Not far away from where Simon lay, Mark Kenton and his children sat down to such a meal. Simon's chair was vacant, but it had been vacant many times before, and no one was really concerned about his absence. When Mark had sent him to borrow the saw, he knew that Simon might be gone all day. When the sun went down, he was sure Simon would come home after his day of hiding from work. But Simon did not come home.

As the sun settled behind the wooded mountain rim and the heavy spring woods were cloaked in dust, Simon stirred from his hiding place. He had fought a battle with his conscience and his instinct for civilized living, and he was now more determined than ever not to turn back. Nagging at his heels was the tormenting fear that he would soon hear the angry cries of his pursuers. By now William Leachman's lifeless body had been found, and his neighbors would be on Simon's trail.

While walking cautiously through the woods, another horrible thought crept into the boy's mind. The Virginia woods were full of snakes. During the first warm days of spring the long brown rattlesnakes were crawling away from their filthy rocklined dens of hibernation. Throughout the whole winter they had lain intertwined with hundreds of their sluggish fellows.

They would be in a bad humor because of the crowding and because of their craving for food to nourish their badly starved bodies. Oldtimers said that a human being could not overcome the bite of an angry snake which had just come from hibernation, because its poison was concentrated during the long winter's sleep.

Time and again Simon's neighbors had been bitten by these monsters. Men harvesting grain often heard a dull whirring near their feet and looked down to discover a rough, scaly head drawn back ready to strike. Women pulling flax screamed, and when the men rushed out, they found a rattlesnake coiled and ready to drive home two vicious poison-laden fangs. Then there were long, sneaking copperheaded moccasins which slid through the grass or over leaf-covered ground without making a sound. A rattlesnake was sporting to the extent that it would give its victim a warning by shaking the long string of rattles on the end of its tail. A copperhead was a coward. It would rear its dull greenish copper body with its poisonous green-tinted belly and attack with quick, ferocious thrusts of its head. Many times a neighbor of the Kentons had been bitten. Sometimes when a man was shucking corn in his crib a rattler in search of rats would strike his hand. Often from under a shock of wheat a rattler or a copperhead would strike an ankle. Most of these victims got well, but some of them died. They all suffered the tortures of death. Simon put one foot ahead of another with extreme caution. He remembered that the woodsmen had said you could smell a snake, and he was carefully on guard.

Simon Kenton seemed to have been born with a keen sense for direction, and when daylight came the morning after his first travel, he had made considerable headway. When the deep-red ball of sun popped up suddenly over the eastern line of woods, he stood eighteen miles from home. He was at Ashby's Gap, gazing back eastward. With a twinge of homesickness he stared hard into the thin blue mist to the east; and years later, recalling that moment, he told members of his family that he could see Mark Kenton's cabin. It sat there in the haze no bigger than a thimble.

CHAPTER 5

A Fugitive

I t was daylight, and Simon was still too near to risk letting anyone see him. Someone would recognize him and he would be captured. He was a pitiful, drenched figure. His clothes were wringing wet from heavy dew of the spring night which had settled down upon the fresh young foliage of the bushes. His feet were wet and galled from the vigorous tramp. Every place where a seam of his coarse clothing touched his body was raw. But most disturbing of all, his long hike had made him beastly hungry. He wondered where he would find food. It was too early in the spring for berries. Not even the best woodsman could capture an animal without a gun or a knife with which to make a snare. There were roots which he could eat, but they supplied little strength, and most of them were nauseating.

At last, after a long and restless day, the sun went down. At first it sank slowly, and then it dropped quickly behind the hills to the west. Again the aching youth pulled himself up from his coarse bough bed and began his second night's journey. He wandered through the woods holding steadfastly to a south-westward course. Heartless branches tore at his clothes as he passed, and occasionally a dew-laden branch with large leaves would slap him squarely in the face. He stumbled over fallen logs and stepped into sinkholes where tree stumps had rotted. Creeks, running flush with cold fresh water of the spring rains, blocked his path, and he was forced to jump or wade them. The going was hard. Simon's westward course took him toward the steep Alleghenies. For miles before he reached the mountain wall itself, he climbed one steep ridge after another of the long, rolling Blue Ridge foothills. Pulling oneself up these ridges was an exhausting task, even when one had a good supply of food and was rested. Only a vigorous, courageous man whose body and muscles were agile and tough could undertake such a journey without food.

Many times Simon Kenton had sat at his father's hearthside and heard old woodsmen tell hair-raising yarns of their experiences in the great woods. They told of how men, when lost in the woods, would lose all sense of direction and wander in a circle for hours. They would blunder around in circles, believing they were going straight ahead, until they perished. Their minds would fail them, and they would be tortured to death by frightening spasms of confusion. There was grave danger of this for Simon. He would become lost and wander in an ever-widening circle until he came on some settler's cabin and be captured. Or he would lose his way and become insane and perish from physical exhaustion and hunger.

Dawn of the second day of the journey came. Simon was completely exhausted. He had almost reached the state, which he had heard woodsmen describe, when it seemed that he must lose his reason. But burning fear of capture made him drag one heavy foot after another. His face was scratched and swollen, and his body felt as if it had been torn into a thousand shreds. His coarse, torn trousers sagged about his shrunken stomach.

Hunger would surely defeat him unless he could get food. It was too early to raid fields and gardens. They had just been planted. If Simon stopped at a settler's cabin and asked for food, someone might recognize him.

The people who did not know him would ask embarrassing questions. They would guess, of course, that he was running away. No boy could put off into the great wilderness without a gun. But Simon's hunger was almost overpowering. Every time he weakened and resolved to seek food at a neighboring cabin, the horrible sight of William Leachman lying at the foot of the board tree with his hair entangled in the thornbush and the bloodstains on his mouth frightened him. The ring of moles around his neck stung him, and he resolved to go on at all costs, even if he came to the point of dropping in his tracks.

He wished settlers all along the frontier were not so everlastingly curious. So seldom did they see a stranger that when one appeared they questioned him to death. They always wanted to know why was he traveling? Where was he going? How far was it? Who was his father? Why did he leave home? How old was he? Where was his gun? How many brothers and sisters did he have? What were the people in his neighborhood doing? What was the news from the government? There was no end to these questions. The backwoodsmen did not mean to be rude; they were starved for news. Their interest in a traveler's private affairs was not malicious. Many times Simon himself had heard his family question a traveler. Everybody who had gone westward was anxious to know what was going on in the older settlements along the eastern seaboard.

It was frightening to be questioned. Simon knew that if he lied to his hearers, he would give himself away. If he told them the truth, he was certain that he would be arrested. More than once his face flushed a deep red when he was unable to give sufficiently vague answers to the questions. Suddenly he came on some men working in a clearing. They saw the boy walking bareheaded in the sun, and one of them gave him a hat. Simon with a great effort did not ask them for food.

On the third day he came to a pole cabin in a small clearing. A wisp of blue smoke drifted up from the chimney top. The door swung open, and Simon could see a fire blazing on the hearth. Two children played about the room, and a woman bent over a bed of coals cooking hoecakes. His head whirled, his whole body trembled with excitement and exhaustion. Perhaps he was far enough from home to escape detection. Surely he could run away if they asked embarrassing questions. He knocked at the door, and the woman gave him some of the hot corn bread she was cooking on the coals. Despite his great hunger, he ate sparingly and returned to his journey.

By the end of the third day Simon took stock of his situation. He had always been mentally alert, and for sixteen years he had escaped work with a reasonable degree of success. Now was a time to be clever, and it would secure him food.

At a cabin he shouldered a hoe and went to work in a cornfield. The family gave him plenty to eat and asked few questions. Simon quickly recovered from his exhaustion and hunger, but every moment he was afraid. Every time a dog barked he was frightened. A cow wandered up outside the cabin at night and he listened, tense for fear an old neighbor would ride up and ask to spend the night. For three days Simon stuck to his job, but on the third day a stranger entered the opposite side of the field. Simon dropped his hoe and fled.

As he traveled farther, distance gave Simon new courage. No longer would he slink through the woods under cover of darkness like a hunted animal. The days of fretfully lying hidden under cover of a bush while he suffered the agony of hunger were over. He had risked using his wits to secure food and shelter, and he would continue to do so.

Simon's new experience taught him that he would have to prepare ahead of time for the grueling encounters with his settler friends. He hit upon the happy idea of creating for himself a new personality. Instead of submitting to all the questioning himself, he would ask questions. He would find out as much as possible about the country and the people who lived in it.

Simon wanted to know especially the name of the man a day's journey away, and when he reached that settler's cabin, he would walk up boldly and introduce himself by the same name. The shrewd backwoods boy knew the frontiersman's passionate love of kinfolk. At every cabin where he stopped, he would proudly proclaim himself a kinsman. This ruse always got him food and shelter, and he interested his hosts in family affairs, and they forgot to ask questions about him.

The runaway boy continued to use this clever trick of securing food and lodging. He knew that a stranger was always welcome if he could stand to be crowded by his bedfellows and bitten by the bugs and fleas. Beds were spread on the floor before the fireplace until all of the space was taken. If there were more sleepers than there were bed accommodations, the overflow was sent up the peg ladder into the corner of the loft overhead. Simon was used to this kind of sleeping arrangement in his father's cabin.

Night after night he sat by the glowing hearth and told stories of the "family" back east, and speculated on his journey westward. His journey was now becoming a high adventure in traveling.

Long ago travelers journeying along the Braddock road toward the Ohio had drifted by the Kenton homestead to tell of their travels. Old soldiers around the campfires, the cornhuskings, house raisings, and logrollings had told of the time they had helped to cut the road. Simon knew about the settlement at the head of the Ohio, and it was to be a jumping-off place into the unexplored wilderness for him.

So, when he had gone more than a hundred and thirty miles

from home, Simon changed his course of travel from a southwestward to a northwestward direction. Instead of going directly toward the towering Appalachian wall which ran through western Virginia, he headed for the fort at the head of the Ohio.

He moved closer and closer to his goal. Each day he changed his name to that of a settler ahead. He arrived one evening at the home of an imaginative and talkative man named Butler. Butler's glowing description of his illustrious ancestry was impressive to the fleeing Simon. Here was a man who was somebody. This boastful talk appealed to Simon's pride. He liked Butler, and he liked his name, and for nine years called himself "Butler."

In his flight westward, Simon was badly handicapped without a gun. He had to have a gun if he was to go on. His "Cousin" Butler agreed to give Simon work until he had earned one. For several weeks he worked with his backwoods host by day and listened to tales of his high-sounding kinfolk by night. Simon fell asleep each night with an increasing sense of security. The choking fear of recognition which had haunted him during the first few nights in the woods was disappearing. Under his new name of Simon Butler, he felt that there was a fair degree of safety. The end of each long, warm day brought him nearer the ownership of better clothes and a precious rifle.

Simon had never owned a rifle. Now that he was on his own and headed westward, a gun was a necessity. As he worked in Butler's grassy crop, he raised his hoe and aimed it at the birds which flew overhead. Butler had promised him a rifle, and already he had his eye on one which hung from the buckhorns over the cabin door. It was a fine gun with a long octagonal barrel and a large bore. The beautifully polished walnut stock and barrel guard were nicely carved. The rifle really was too heavy for so young a boy to hold up to his shoulder and fire. But the notch on the end of the stock fitted Simon's shoulder perfectly, and if need be, he could fire it from a rest.

It was a grand feeling to sit before the cabin with the rifle across his lap. Simon could hardly wait for the moment when the gun would be his. He would ram home a load of powder, and cram a lead ball in on top of it with the strong hickory ramrod, and fire it just to hear it roar.

Late one afternoon as Simon walked home from the field behind his host, Butler said, "Well, Simon, we are through hoeing. I think you have done enough work to pay for the clothes and the rifle." This was good news. Simon was a free man. Ownership of the rifle gave him a sense of importance. He was transformed into a man of the woods, and he was ready to resume his journey.

Near Warm Springs, Simon Butler fell in with a man named Johnson. Johnson was a mysterious New Jerseyman who gave evidence of traveling through the wilderness, like Simon, to bury his troubles. There was a bond of kinship between the two because of an unexpressed something back home, and they joined forces. This new friend had a pack horse loaded with provisions, and he and Simon killed game along the way to supply fresh meat which they cooked over open campfires. It was a grand life. Never before had Simon felt so free and independent. The two travelers moved quickly, and within an unreasonably short time they were at Ise's Ford on the Cheat River. Here Butler and Johnson parted company.

At this new frontier settlement Simon Butler found some new and exciting friends. John Mahon and his brother, Jacob Greathouse, and William Grills were preparing for a big hunting expedition in the great woods along the Ohio River. They were busily engaged in making a canoe and repairing their rifle stocks. Gunlocks were oiled and tightened, fuse holes were picked clean. Flints were carefully selected and fastened in place. The tiny pans which held the powder that would receive the spark when the flint rasped down beside the lock were scraped clean. A hunter going into the woods knew well that his gun had to work perfectly or there would be a gruesome end to his life.

Hundreds of tales were told along the frontier of a hunter whose flints had flashed in the pan and failed to explode the charge of powder tamped in the butt of the gun's barrel. A bear had snatched the rifle from the luckless hunter's hand and then pummeled him to death, or an Indian had driven an arrow home and walked off with the white man's scalp dangling from his belt.

Sacks of meal and parched corn were packed away in the canoe so they would not get damp in the journey downstream. Into the tight corner of the bow where no harm would come to it, went a precious buckskin pouch of alum salt. Long bone-handled skinning knives were sharpened to razor keenness and were placed in soft leather holders. Moccasins, leather breeches, and elkskin hunting coats were put in condition. Older hunters worked and told of their experiences in the woods of the Ohio Valley. Few people had ever hunted there. Game was plentiful. Bears roamed through the canebrakes, their huge brown sides rolling with fat. Deer were as common as gray squirrels in the Virginia woods, and turkeys almost as numerous as mosquitoes. The big sport, however, came while hunting buffalo and elk. There was one drawback: the hunting ground was claimed by jealous Indians. They stalked hunting camps of the whites, and many times a huddle of green bones smoldering in a campfire told their own horrible story of a hunter who had been ambushed.

The four hunters were glad to have Simon for a companion. Five men made an ideal hunting party. Although Simon was only sixteen, he took a man's place in the hunting party.

Hustling around to get ready for the long trip was exciting to Simon, and momentarily he forgot about William Leachman.

The moles around his neck ceased to sting him; he was happy.

Simon and his companions planned to go down the Cheat to the Monongahela, and down the Monongahela to the Ohio River. Simon Butler was thrilled to know that he was about to embark upon such high adventure.

CHAPTER 6

Down The Ohio

At last the Cheat River hunters were ready to depart for the Ohio. Members of the party were astir, and they broke camp before the sun was up. A man sat in each end of the long skin canoe and one on each of the three cross seats in the body of the boat.

The canoe was an interesting vessel. The hunters had built a sturdy framework of hickory and willow. Each end was drawn into a sharp point and a piece of seasoned hickory fastened in place as a bumper strip. Wide spring midribs formed a deep belly for freight. Over the bulging frame dried and scraped deerskins were laced tightly into place. When Simon and his companions finished their crude canoe, it was not a beautiful craft, but it was fitted to their use.

When at last the canoe was afloat, the men discovered that the current of the Cheat ran fast and strong. Occasionally it eddied in a wild maelstrom around the heavy boulders which divided the stream, or it piled up in a thin roaring wall around the sharp bends where rocky shoulders reared themselves out of the water.

It passed through a wild, unbroken country where the steep ridges lifted themselves up to tremendous heights above the river's edge. When the gray mist drifted upward in midmorning and wide bands of sunlight filtered underneath, Simon could see the huge forest-covered shelves which tumbled back in deeply broken lines from the shores.

With quick, deep strokes, the carefree hunters tugged at their long oars. They dodged boulders and steered clear of treacherous eddies that would have broken their flimsy craft in two in a single violent whirl. Simon shouted and sang, and his voice rebounded from the towering, rocky cliffsides in weird staccato rumblings. From the mouth of the Cheat, the party steered down the wider Monongahela to the broad Ohio. Running the river was a thrilling experience for Simon. Without realizing that he was working, the boy had dug his oar into the water in long vigorous strokes.

On the way, but before his rollicking party could reach the Ohio, Simon was to get his first realistic taste of the border Indian menace. David Duncan, an Indian trader, came through the woods to tell the Mahon brothers that their father was still alive. He had been captured a short time before by the Indians, and his sons had given him up for dead. Duncan's report broke up the hunting expedition.

Simon was badly disappointed to have his plans ruined. He and his companions had gone to such pains to prepare for their journey, and now it was all in vain. Where Simon had been happy a day before, he was now despondent. Again he was left alone to make his way into the western country.

When Simon's companions were gone, he wandered into the settlement of Provence and for a time worked for his board and keep and looked for new companions to go with him into the wilderness on a hunting trip.

In Provence, Simon came on two interesting frontier characters. One was a mature man named "Long Dutchman" George Yeager, who could speak several Indian languages. He had been captured when a baby by the Indians and had lived among them for several years. The other was George Strader, a young boy from the western settlements of Pennsylvania, who, like Simon Kenton, was seeking adventure in the great woods. These two were of German origin. Their people had immigrated to eastern Pennsylvania and then had moved westward across the frontier.

For days Simon and George Strader sat and listened to Yeager's long, exciting stories concerning the rich caneland to be found on the lower Ohio River, where the tall cane grew in billowing brakes of thousands of acres. It was called "Kaintucke." Many times the Long Dutchman had been there with his Indian captors, and had hunted with them for weeks at a time. They had waded through the paths which penetrated the heavy canes and had spent many anxious hours on the broad buffalo roads and around the boggy salt licks looking for game. Buffalo herds, numbering thousands of animals, had plodded along the wide, dust-strewn trails which entered Kentucky from the Ohio. Fleet elk bucks led large herds of nervous does along these routes. There were scores of bears, and in the late evenings and the dead of night one could hear the bloodcurdling screams of the panther and the mournful howl of hungry wolves.

All a hunter had to do in this wonderland was to seat himself beside a broad, dusty trail and wait for game. These trails were deep-padded highways worn smooth by centuries of travel. They connected one salt lick with another and with the vast central Kentucky grazing ground.

No one knows when the first buffalo began to graze in this region. One thing is well known, however, the buffalo road builders were masters at locating a right of way. They eliminated all unnecessary climbs uphill and all wading across treacherous bogs. Stocky bulls led their herds in a loping pace overland. Their heads were carried close to the ground ahead of their heavy wool-coated shoulders. A short, rigid horn jutted out from each side of the head, and beady black eyes looked out from under shaggy brows. To shoot one of these charging beasts was real sport; a hunter had to aim carefully. If a bullet lodged in a shoulder or glanced off, the hunter had to be ready to get out of the way in a hurry. Buffalo meat was good. The tongue especially was a delicacy when roasted over a bed of live coals. The deep-red steaks cut from the heavy haunches and shoulders were temptation enough to make a hunter risk his life to down one of the big bulls.

After the tongue and select steaks had been cut away, the rest of the meat was used for jerking. The heavy black hide was valuable. A skilled woodsman could cure it and make from it both a bed and cover for his half-faced camp. A well-cured buffalo skin was even warmer than the huge feather beds which the more industrious women back in the settlements made from goose feathers. Simon knew about the comforts of skin coverings. Back in the Virginia settlements children argued on cold nights as to who would sleep under the heavy bear- and deerskins. In many instances the skins were held in such high affection by the families that they were given names.

Elk followed the trails to the canebrakes and the salt licks. They were shy, sensitive animals. Their long, graceful legs were mounted over razor-sharp hoofs. Their movement through the cane was the most graceful of any animal in the wilderness.

Where the buffalo galloped over the trail in a tail-switching lope, the elk held itself erect. Its head was always up, and its pointed nose and large brown eyes were ever on the alert. The proud males were adorned for most of the year with widespreading antlers. The elk was the proudest member of the entire deer family. To bag one was a feather in any hunter's cap. It provided the best winter meat to be found in the great woods, and many a hunter pulled himself through a lean hunting season with a winter supply of jerked elk.

Yeager remembered that numerous trails crisscrossed Kentucky. There were many barren licks where the grazing animals congregated to get salt. Far beneath the earth's surface in the limestone country were wide fissures in the rock stratae, and a salt brine was forced upward by pressure to flavor large plots of ground. One of the most famous places and one of the important animal crossroads was Big Bone Lick. Its miry bed was lined with huge bones of the artic elephant which had ventured south centuries ago to get salt. The clumsy bodies of these mammoths had sunk in the ooze and they had perished. There were bones so large that a company of surveyors, stopping there in a later year, used rib bones for tent poles and the wide shoulder bones for seats.

Deeper in Kentucky country were the Upper and Lower Blue Licks and scores of others, where first the Indians and meat-eating animals gathered to prey upon the buffalo, deer, and elk. Young George Yeager had sat with his dusky captors about these same Kentucky licks. He could call up within his imagination the thunderous sound of the milling buffalo licking frantically at the savory ground. He remembered vividly the cautious approach of the deer and elk, the slinking movement in the brush of the grunting brown bears. Panthers and wolves had screamed and howled a short distance away, waiting to make a kill. All this had excited the white boy, and created within him an undying love for the woods. As he sat there now in Provence, it all seemed the fantastic dream of a land of unreality. There were many other adventures which came home to George Yeager as he and his companions worked diligently to get ready for their journey downstream to search for the caneland. He was reveling in the memory and the retelling of these yarns. He was pleased to see with what enthusiasm Kenton and Strader listened. George had waited many months for an opportunity to go in search of this fertile country. He needed sturdy companions who would undergo, without complaint, the hardships of the woods, until they could find Kentucky.

Here were companions for Simon, to replace the expedition that had just failed. Simon was now anxious to venture deep into the western woods. Already the ties with home were severed, and he wanted to travel on westward.

Again Simon was forced to help build and equip a canoe. Like Grills, Greathouse, and the Mahon brothers, the three adventurers took special care with their preparations. They tried to avoid any accident that might be due to carelessness. Their guns were rubbed clean and oiled. Coarse Indian meal was stored in a waterproof pouch, and corn was parched and salted. A bag of alum salt for the meat and coarse journeycakes was packed away in a safe, dry place. Bundles of flaxen tow and fluffy feathers were put in each hunting bag to be used in cleaning the guns. Powder bags were filled, and leaden balls were run from the little hand molds. Tomahawks were sharpened to a razor edge and fitted with strong hickory handles. Knives were carefully prepared and holstered at the end of leather shoulder straps. Yeager said it was a long journey down the Ohio, and even the best-equipped party would have trouble making the trip without mishap. One bit of neglect in preparation for such a journey would mean defeat.

At last Simon and his companions completed their preparations. The heavily laden canoe splashed headlong into the river, and before long it was gliding rapidly toward the big basin where the Monongahela and Allegheny rivers came together to form the Ohio. Above this junction sat Fort Pitt, a famous landmark on the western frontier. This had been a goal for General Braddock's troops, and later in the French and Indian War it was an important factor in the military campaigns of both the French and the British. Many times Simon had heard of this post as a jumping-off place for men who entered the great wilderness by way of the Ohio River. Fort Pitt had been Simon's vague destination when he set off into the woods after his fight with William Leachman. As he and his companions turned their canoe about to enter the Ohio, Simon was anxious to get a good look at the settlement. He raised himself up to look back at the sprawling outpost of white civilization which crowned the rocky tongue of land hemmed in by the junction of the three rivers.

Immediately below Fort Pitt, long before the canoe had drifted out of sight of the mist-covered fort, the boatmen began to realize that they were rapidly slipping past the line of white settlement. To Simon, who had shuddered many times during the last few weeks at thoughts of capture and the hangman's noose, civilized Virginia seemed now to be on another continent. The river straightened out a bit into long, sweeping bends. Tall hardwood trees with their heavy, spreading branches crowded up to the shoulders of the stream. Down at the river's edge water-loving trees crowded in and stretched long, bushy branches far out over the water in a greedy effort to choke off human passage. From where Simon sat, low in the canoe, and looked back upstream, he got the impression that the Ohio River rolled through a soft carpet of green forest.

As Yeager steered the canoe with the fast, drifting current, the three hunters became more and more conscious of the uncertainties which cropped up in a man's mind as he passed beyond the limits of civilization. They were being swept rapidly into a country where they would have to meet heartless natural conditions with their own feeble, individual resources. They now had to stand or fall on their ability to fight back at the savage forces that would block their paths.

Few white men had passed that way. French fur traders and, occasionally, frontier French officials had moved silently up and down the rivers of the West in their long, dark canoes. The Ohio had appealed to their artistic fancies, and out of their love for it they called the river "La Belle Riviere." Celeron de Bienville had traveled down the Ohio on his way from Quebec to New Orleans to bury the famous leaden plates which were to betoken French ownership of the land. Before him the adventurous La Salle had traveled over part of it. A few hardy Virginians had crossed the eastern mountain barrier and had made the journey by water.

Most famous of the early adventurers was Chistopher Gist, who went down the Ohio to Kentucky four years before Simon Kenton was born. He had come west as a scout for an ambitious land company which was seeking to run far ahead of the line of settlement and to lay claim to fertile land for future speculation.

Gist's trip as a land-staking venture was a failure, because he had turned back before he reached his destination. He had seen, however, many Indians at Logstown where Portsmouth, Ohio, now stands. George Crogan, an Indian trader, had given him much useful information, and one of Crogan's men had gone with him to the Big Bone Lick. Gist had gone home to tell of the virgin land he had visited. His tall tales of his travels westward were repeated from mouth to mouth and years later led to the migration of many Virginia settlers.

The next year Lewis Evans came west in the employ of the British crown. He had been sent out to make a map of the Ohio River. Again, in 1754, Gist was back on the Ohio, this time as the guide for young George Washington. Washington came as an agent for the English government seeking an understanding with the French, who were building forts along the great river.

Before the canoe the scene changed constantly, as the Ohio spread out in broad, sweeping curves. The ridges below Fort Pitt did not crowd the river into sharp turns as they did farther downstream. As the canoe was swept along with the current,

George Yeager, from his seat in the stern, became woodsmaster. During idle days of floating, he instructed his young companions in the meticulous art of woodcraft.

In Simon Kenton and George Strader he found two apt pupils. Yeager, because of his many hunting expeditions with the Indians, knew well the many precautions a woodsman had to take.

In the cane country of Kentucky they would have to match wits with both Indians and clever animals. Yeager remembered vividly the many bitter fights which had taken place among the Indians of the various tribes for possession of this vast hunting ground. The tribes from the south claimed the land, and the tribes from the north disputed their claims bitterly.

Time and again maddened warriors had taken to the warpath to rescue their land from their rivals. So often had they gone to war over this country that deep warriors' trails had been beaten across it.

Every trespasser was an enemy. The white man was a dangerous invader, and Indians from both sides shot him at sight on general principles. Too well the Indians knew what the appearance of the white man in the caneland meant. With deep misgivings, they had watched him push back their hunting grounds before the growing settlements east of the mountains.

CHAPTER 7

Hunting With Yeager

Throughout the western woods, there were angry Indians ready to smear gaudy war paint over their long, bony faces. Even as Simon's long canoe pitched forward in the billowing Ohio current, braves watched from the banks. Occasionally the boys spotted a brown face staring at them. Every time a branch quivered, Simon was up on his knees with his cocked rifle, sure it was Indians. It was not that he was frightened, but rather that he looked forward to a quick brush with the natives.

While Simon and his companions were riding deep into the woods, the braves sat about the council fires and pounded the war club heavily upon the ground in voting for resistance against all invaders.

Knowledge of this bitterness called for extreme caution against discovery. The art of self-preservation in the woods was a difficult one. Woodsmen wore moccasins, partly because they seldom left a deep telltale footprint and partly because they were easy to make with a knife and a wooden lacing needle from skins cured in the woods. A man could walk through fallen leaves without making a sound or without leaving a trail of upturned leaves and thus exposing his path by damp spots. He had to learn to lift his feet clear of the ground and set them down squarely on top of the leaves. In passing through the underbrush the hunter had to use great caution to avoid breaking branches or leaving the grayish sides of leaves turned up. He avoided knocking off bits of bark, and never did he succumb to the great temptation of hacking trees with his tomahawk.

If a woodsman must be skilled at covering up his own trail, he likewise needed skill in discovering a trail left by others. He had to be able to discover and interpret both animal and Indian signs. The footprint of an animal contained a story within itself. The experienced hunter could tell quickly what kind of animal made the track, which direction it was traveling, whether it was traveling slowly or had been stampeded into a run. A careful examination of the track indicated how long ago the print had been made. A scattered heap of leaves might have a slightly unnatural appearance. By moving them back carefully, it would be found that they covered the ashes of a campfire. To know these things brought success; ignorance of them brought certain failure.

Weather conditions governed hunting. On warm, sunny days grazing animals waded deep into the cool valleys and low plains. When the weather was threatening, they climbed upward, and on stormy days they took cover under cliffs and in heavy timber.

A hunter had to determine the direction in which the wind was blowing before stalking a herd of buffalo, elk, or deer; to approach game downwind was folly. Before the hunter could get within gunshot, a nervous buck would throw up his head and snort a warning and gallop the herd off in the opposite direction.

Traveling through the vast and strange woods without a compass was difficult. At night a hunter could find his way by following the stars. In daytime there was one certain guide: bark and moss on the north side of the trees grew thicker and coarser. The flow of the streams sometimes indicated a specific location.

Food was always a problem. Man had a natural taste for bread; without it, eating became a trying thing. Hunters went to the western woods with precious bags of meal and parched corn. Meal was given great care because it had a tendency to mold. Parched corn would retain its crispness and freshness longer than any other type of food the hunter could take with him. Fresh meat was not always available, and in cold winter months much of the game was too poor to be used for food.

To prepare for cold months, hunters jerked their supplies of meat. The fresh red haunches of buffalo, deer, and elk were cut into thin strips and hung in the sun to dry. They were smoked until cured and richly flavored over a hardwood fire.

Jerked meat would keep as long as the outer crust was kept hard and dry. It was fine for packing through the woods. A hunter cut off bits of it to chew as he walked along. When bread became scarce, many hunters killed turkeys and cooked the white dry meat of the breast as a substitute. There was real art in preparing luscious venison steaks over a bed of hot coals. Simon learned how to do this, and he learned how to cook corn bread in a bed of ashes.

In dressing game, great care was used to create as little disturbance of the surroundings as possible. Blood and offal were buried. The skin was rolled tightly and lodged safe above the ground. The meat in large hunks or quarters was hung in the open out of reach of wolves and bears.

A man dressed in a drab deerskin hunting suit had to be careful not to stand before a dark tree; above all, he had to avoid the trees with white boles, such as the sycamore. The art of concealing oneself behind a tree was an exact one. Seldom could a woodsman choose the best tree to hide behind. Emergencies arose and a cornered man had to use the tree nearest him.

Sometimes the trees were small, and the woodsman had to know which part of his body to conceal and which part to expose. A bullet or an arrow through the fatty parts of the hips caused a painful wound, but it perhaps would not prove fatal. A wound in the chest, however, was dangerous. The hunter caught out in the open had to make himself appear to be a stump, or he had to drop flat on the ground to hide in the leaves.

There were thousands of sounds in the woods, and a woodsman had to learn all of them. A buffalo cow called to her calf, and there was a certain tremor or overtones in the call which could not be imitated. The bulls bellowed to each other. Turkey gobblers broke the stillness of the early morning with their thunderous gobbling and the drumming of their stiff wing feathers over their shins. Squirrels ran up and down the hickory and chestnut trees barking and scratching. Woodpeckers hammered away on dead tree trunks and uttered their sharp impulsive calls. A quail sitting quiet on the lower branch of a bush whistled "bobwhite" in clear round tones, and the hens answered back in lonesome single-note calls. Owls screamed into the stillness of the night with their startling hoots, and occasionally they uttered unnerving babbles of sounds in concert.

From the canebrakes long-eared and big-toothed buck rabbits cut the young canes and slapped their front feet together as they uttered weird whistles.

There were thousands of other animal and insect sounds. A good woodsman had to have an ear for all of them. It was not enough to be able to identify them, he had to know them so well that he could tell when they were off key. Hunters and settlers alike had often mistaken an Indian imitating the gobble of a turkey and had met death.

Yeager was a good teacher. He prepared Simon and Strader in the arts of the woods which he in turn had learned from the Indians. His captivity had prepared him admirably for the rugged life of the great hunting ground.

Simon Kenton had learned many of the elementary things about living in the woods as a child back in Virginia. On his hunting trips around his father's cabin, he had learned much of the art of creeping upon game and had come to know many of the sounds of the woods. Mark Kenton had been a close observer of the weather, and many of these facts Simon already knew. George Yeager's teachings in woodcraft were of an advanced nature. George taught the boys the things they had to know and use when there were no civilized settlements to which they could go.

When Simon and his companions were far down the river, Yeager began searching for familiar landmarks. Above them on the high river bluff was a long line of timber. One after another, tiny stream mouths bit their way through the rocky barricade to the big river.

At Cabin Creek just above the mouth of the Limestone, the three hunters peered into the mouth of the wide opening which led up the great bluff. They did not know it was the head of a famous game trail that led directly over the hill to the caneland they were seeking.

Lower down, Big Bone Creek poured its waters from underneath a heavy stand of willows and sycamores. There was something familiar about the country, yet Yeager could not be certain that he had seen it before. Before the canoe had reached that place on the Ohio where the land spread out on both sides into low, flat bottoms, Yeager was hopelessly confused. In his mind back at Provence he had a perfect picture of the country, but now it was all a maze of confusion. Nothing seemed to fit into his memory. At last the canoe was swung around in the wide mouth of the Kentucky. On the corner of land between the river's mouth and the Ohio, they found the initials of James McBride, which had been carved there in 1754. But nowhere did the hunters see canebrakes.

It was heartbreaking to travel so far by canoe and then to miss the magic land. Yeager was pitiful in his frustration. The three men reached a quick decision. They had spent many weeks in traveling downstream. Summer had passed quickly into fall, and now the days were shorter. Cold breezes were sweeping down the river. Winter was coming, and they would have to build a hunting camp. They turned back upstream to establish winter quarters. As they tugged at their oars going back, they searched diligently for a clue that would lead them to Kaintucke. They stopped at the mouths of Licking River, Bracken, Killikinic, Cabin, Limestone, and Big Sandy creeks, but they found no cane.

Not far from the mouth of the Big Sandy, upstream on the Ohio, was the Great Kanawha. Its sheltering bluffs made an ideal place for a winter camp and the woodsmen could stalk enough game to supply their food, and they could ramble to their hearts' content in the unbroken woods. Here, ten miles from the banks of the Ohio, they made camp and prepared for winter.

Their first task was to build a good stout hunter's lean-to or an open-faced lodge. A heavy backlog was placed across the rear and staked down so that it could not roll out of place. Two forked stakes were braced against each other as corner uprights, and long brace poles were laid from these forks down to the base log. Long rafters were laid across these. A roof of elm, hemlock, and hickory bark was placed over the rafters. If the weather became too bad, leaves and dirt would be thrown over the slanting roof to help turn the water. The ends were enclosed with bark and skins, with the wide front left open. A heap of dirt was piled all the way across the front for a fireplace.

Night after night the hunters dragged long green logs from the woods to pile on the fire. Heaps of red coals were used to cook Johnnycakes and to broil luscious venison steaks. When the wind blew hard and the temperature fell rapidly, the fire was kept burning all night to take the chill off the air in the lean-to. After many a day's tramp in the woods, the three men came back to camp with their feet soaking wet. It was an old rule of the woods for a man to bake his feet by the fire at night. The fire was supposed to draw off the poison which caused the pain of rheumatism.

Yeager used all his keen knowledge of the woods, and for more than a year his choice of campsite was a happy one. It was the kind of place where the passage of time meant nothing. Back of the camp was a wide valley in which the three hunters found deer and elk, bear, panthers, and turkeys. Along the nearby streams was an abundance of fur-bearing animals. Quickly the woodsmen realized that they could buy their supplies by running a trapline. With axes and knives they made deadfalls and snares, and with broad boards for shovels they dug deep pits in which to catch bears, wolves, and turkeys.

The western land was free, and no one was there to compete for the hunting. So completely were Kenton, Yeager, and Strader removed from civilization that the affairs of their hunting camp were hardly governed by units of time. Long, lazy fall days shortened gradually into those of winter. The fire blazed higher and longer each night. But freedom of the land remained constant. A man could lie abed all day, or he could arise and take to the trail as early as he pleased. This was a glorious life for Simon. He had never been happy under the restrictive rules of a community. To him the keen enjoyment of life was measured by the sunshine, the snow, the woods, and the game which wandered in them. The most glorious experience a man ever had was that of stretching himself upon the ground, flat on his back, and dozing until he was ready to take to the trail again. This was freedom—freedom with just enough work and excitement attached to prevent boredom.

Simon delighted in the sport of outwitting wily animals. Early in his youth he had not found hunting an attractive sport, but here, where he matched his wits against those of sensitive animals, he found enjoyment. Month after month he wandered through the woods laughing and bantering Yeager and Strader. He and Strader put into practice the things Yeager had taught them on their canoe trip down the Ohio earlier in the year. Rapidly the clever art of woodcraft was becoming second nature with him as was proved by the increasing cache of furs and skins.

Winter and spring came and passed on into summer. Simon scarcely noticed his seventeenth birthday. A year had gone by since he beat William Leachman into a state of unconsciousness, but now he was safe from capture deep in the western Virginia woods. Only one need faced the hunters, their supply of gunpowder and lead was almost exhausted. Long ago they had eaten the last of their cornmeal. The salt pouch was empty, and unsalted meat was not appetizing. They packed their skins into a canoe and went down to the Ohio. There a passing Indian trader sold them new supplies for their pelts, and life again took on a bright outlook.

Once more the three adventurers plunged into the woods to hunt. The summer and fall passed quickly. Occasionally they came across Indian signs. Simon had come to know some of the Indians of the Kanawha Valley, and their relationship was friendly.

Occasionally a party of Indians came over the river to wander in the Virginia woods, and sometimes Simon and his companions would come back to camp to discover that they had passed close by. But this was natural. Indians had always crossed the big river to hunt in these woods.

As Indian signs increased, there seemed to be more activity on the part of the white man on the Ohio. During good weather canoes bearing white land hunters and traders pushed quietly underneath the sheltering branches of the trees which spread out from the water's edge. Or they stood out in bold relief in the middle of the stream.

Simon, Yeager, and Strader were ignorant of happenings east of the mountains. Every year a huddle of new cabins marked the beginning of another spreading island of settlement. Population in the eastern states grew rapidly. Land in the older communities became poorer after the harvest of each crop and winter's erosion. It was said that a man planted the land four years, and the fifth he turned it back to nature and moved elsewhere to clear some more. Taxes were high in the old settlements, and tightfisted landlords extracted exorbitant rents from tenants. To the west, land was "free for the taking." A man could take his tomahawk into the woods and blaze a line around a plot of ground and call it his own. Many a householder loaded what goods he could on two or three pack horses and set out for the western woods.

Everywhere in western Pennsylvania, Virginia, and Carolina, restlessness was making itself felt in long strings of frontier emigrants. Colonial officials created friction, and headstrong Irish, Scotch, and German settlers moved away. Fort Pitt was growing rapidly into a populous community. Cabins were springing up far beyond the walls of the stockades. Every month there were newcomers. Occasionally a venturesome family moved a short way down the Ohio to build a cabin and grow a patch of corn.

CHAPTER 8

Winter Camp

Far to the southwest, white settlements were spreading also. Two years before Simon Kenton had left home, James Robertson and John Sevier, two bold young men of southeastern Virginia, led settlers into the rich Watauga Valley to establish a new settlement there almost under the shadow of the Allegheny wall. That same year Daniel Boone and John Finley with a party of hunters had slipped silently through the great Cumberland Gap to hunt in Yeager's wild Kentucky caneland.

Kentucky country was a glorious place indeed for Boone. Never before had this romantic woodsman seen such a country. With the soul of a true poet, Boone wished to spend the rest of his life there. Days, weeks, and months went by. Summer became Indian summer, and fall became winter. Finley and the others wished to go home, but Daniel Boone could not bring himself to leave the wilderness paradise. Not even a wife and children back east of the mountains were enough of an attraction to take him away. With persuasive earnestness he got his brother Squire and two other hunters to remain with him. Even when tragedy stalked their camp and the two hunters were killed, Daniel and Squire continued their hunting. On two occasions when supplies ran low, Squire went back to North Carolina, but Daniel remained in Kentucky. He was intoxicated with the land.

Other white men came overland to hunt. A party of men came from the Yadkin and Holston valleys to roam for months. Their sturdy old German guide, Kaspar Mansker, led them through Cumberland Gap to the fertile plains of the present Bluegrass of Kentucky. Once while on this trip, they had come on Daniel Boone sprawled on his back singing at the top of his voice in the midst of a canebrake.

Across the mountains to the east other things were happening which were to affect the great woods of the West. Land-hungry speculators were planning to secure large grants of the colonial lands. Their agents had been going west since 1750, when Dr. Thomas Walker had passed through Cumberland Gap.

A year later Christopher Gist had gone down the Ohio on a similar mission. Again the land agents were coming west, and they were not too diplomatic in their treatment of the Indians. Already a dispute had been started with the Cherokees as to who owned lands in western Virginia.

Beyond the Ohio the braves were becoming excited. The war club was passing menacingly from hand to hand on many questions of tribal policy. Worried chiefs delivered long and eloquent harangues to their tribesmen. Angry warriors came away from the council fires to roam the woods and inflict quick vengeance upon white poachers.

Rapidly the Ohio River frontier was becoming the center of violence between the whites and their Indian neighbors. Cut off from civilization, Kenton, Yeager, and Strader were ignorant of the rapidly approaching storm. The fall days of 1772 passed as had those of the year before. Looking up to the tall ridges around him and down through the long curving valleys, it seemed to Simon that no manmade troubles would ever invade the woods.

Winter came on, and snow drifted against the lean-to. The hunters turned their moccasins skin side in and pulled heavy skin caps down around their ears.

Again, flames from the big fire leaped high into the air to temper the biting cold. A trap line had been established to catch furs to exchange for supplies in the spring. January and February were cold months, and March had come in with a heavy snowfall. Early that month Simon and John Strader went out to run the trap line, while Yeager remained behind to clean and stretch skins. All day the two boys trudged through the heavy snow. Their feet and legs shivered in the porous moccasins and leggings. The sharp crust of the snow gouged at their shins, and the brisk wind froze their hands and faces. Late in the afternoon they trudged into camp.

Before the camp, long, red tongues of flame from the green-log fire leaped high into the air. Yeager's sturdy body was outlined in the broad opening of the shelter. Simon and John were glad to get back to such a warm welcome. Quickly they ate their supper and stripped the steaming moccasins and breeches from their bodies. They were dead tired and ready for the bed. The weary hunters had hardly pulled the heavy buffalo robes up under their chins before a shot rang out. Indians had at last found their camp, and now they were hemmed in by a band of warriors lying in ambush. In long jumps Kenton and Strader reached the woods. They were barefooted and clad only in their shirts. Yeager was wounded. In his headlong rush for cover, Simon had looked back and seen Yeager hold out a hand and take one step toward the Indians. He could hear Yeager's voice uttering Shawnee words of friendship.

Simon and John Strader found each other in the woods. They were glad to be free, but they were afraid they would never see the wise and companionable George Yeager again. Doubtless he was taken prisoner, and perhaps he would die a torturous death at the stake, his flesh and bones turning to ashes in a council house over the Ohio.

Simon trod barefoot through the woods in disgust. He mumbled criticism of himself to Strader. "Hit jest don't make sense, George," he said. "We didn't use no sense at all. Here we been sleeping all year with our guns in easy reach, and the first time we needed them we run off without them like a pair of scared deer." Simon's conscience hurt him. "We let George get taken prisoner without raising a finger to help him."

It saddened Simon to think of their companion's falling a prisoner to the Indians. But it was likewise tragic that the two boys had lost their clothing and guns. Simon lost the long rifle which he had worked so hard to earn from his "Cousin" Butler.

For four days Simon and Strader wandered in a roundabout way through the frozen woods toward the Ohio. Hunger came quickly. There was no way for the helpless boys to secure food. No fruit clung to the barren shrubs. Nuts and roots were buried under the encrusted snow.

By the third day they were almost exhausted. The cold was becoming unbearable. Their feet, hardened by many long days of hiking on the trail and nights of baking before campfires, were now badly cut and bleeding.

Six miles from the Ohio, the weakened boys could no longer stand erect. They dropped to all fours in an effort to travel. Simon's stout heart was weakening. He hardly dared look at Strader for fear his flagging courage would show in his face and cause the other to give up. At sunset they were only a mile from their goal, but they were unable to travel this short distance to the river without rest. Before the sun was up the next day, the boys dragged their emaciated and bruised bodies over the heartless snow for the last mile. Every inch gained was deadly torture. Simon was now calling on every ounce of reserve strength.

Below them, at the foot of the long slope, was a shiny stretch of river. A haunting fear crept into their troubled minds. Would they ever reach the water? Their strength was failing rapidly. And if they did reach it, would they find help? It seemed they could drag their bleeding knees and hands no farther. At that moment they discovered a freshly broken sugar trail. Help must be near. Not far away stood a crude pole cabin with thin wisps of smoke curling upward from its chimney. The exhausted boys were taken in by the kind settler, warmed, clothed, and fed.

Several traders were there, among them Kenton's old friends, William Grills, Jacob Greathouse, and the Mahon brothers. Simon decided to throw in his lot with them again. Because of the Indian raid, the traders moved to the Little Kanawha where there was less danger of raids. John Strader here left the woods, and there is no record to show that he and Kenton ever saw each other again. At the upriver station Simon met a Dr. Briscoe, who employed him during the early spring months as hunter for his party of surveyors. Briscoe's activity took place in the period when scores of anxious settlers were piling into Fort Pitt. Almost every month a party loaded its worldly goods onto flatboats and set sail for the downriver claims. Around the campfires the talk turned more and more to land speculation. Already several parties in the employ of such speculators had gone down the river in search of fertile lands.

There was a great need for experienced scouts. Simon was young, but he had had a man's experience in the woods. He accepted an invitation to become a member of a party that was going to the Falls of the Ohio, under the leadership of Dr. Woods and Hancock Lee, to join Captain Thomas Bullitt's party of land speculators at the mouth of the Scioto. From there they intended to go to the Falls, where Bullitt hoped to found a settlement that would establish claim to a large block of land in Kentucky.

As Dr. Woods's party moved slowly downstream, surveyors were sent ashore to examine the land along the way. At Three Islands they stopped for several days. As the party advanced down the river, Indian signs had become more numerous. The woods were full of warriors, and the signs they left behind them indicated that they were bold. Woods and Lee were afraid to proceed because they were not sufficiently armed to withstand a heavy attack, and to go on would perhaps result in the party's destruction. After discussing the matter, it was decided to give up the journey and turn back toward home. Below Three Islands the party abandoned its canoes and set out overland for Greenbrier County in Virginia.

Traveling in the rugged mountain country was difficult. The party had to cross the steep western ridges from the Big Sandy to the Kanawha and then to the Monongahela and Cheat valleys. Hot weather was exhausting, and it was difficult to secure food for so large a party. Before the men had been on the trail many days, Dr. Woods was bitten by a copperhead moccasin. They established a camp and for two weeks the restless and worn men were forced to wait for their leader to recover.

Every day Simon went to the woods to secure meat for the surveyors. Indian signs were becoming more numerous, and hunting was a ticklish business. One careless mistake and the whole party would be murdered. If the camp was raided, certainly Dr. Woods and perhaps all the others would be made prisoners. If they were not captured immediately, they would be scattered through the woods to be tracked down and killed, or they would perish from hunger and exposure. Simon was called upon not only to be a hunter but to assume the role of guide and guardian of the party.

When Dr. Woods was ready to travel again, the surveyors crossed the mountains to the headwaters of the Monongahela. Not far away were the frontier settlements in Virginia. Within a few days they would be at home. The temptation to go on was great for Simon. He stood and watched his companions disappear in the woods. A wave of homesickness swept over him, but still he remembered the moles around his neck. He had received no news from Virginia, and until he knew what had happened, he felt it best to remain in the woods. He built a canoe and returned to the Kanawha and the scene of his happy year with Yeager and Strader. Later in the year he again joined a party made up of Grills, Greathouse, and the Mahons. They hunted during the remainder of the summer and the fall. Again Simon was able to enjoy the thrill of the great woods.

CHAPTER 9

White Man And Indian At War

The scene along the Ohio was rapidly changing. Lone settlers were building their cabins westward from the Monongahela. Along the Ohio cabins were being built within sight of each other. The village of Wheeling was taking form, and no longer was the upper river a long, solitary stream crowded in upon by unbroken wooded shores.

With the building of each new settler's cabin there was a growing spirit of rivalry among selfish groups. At Williamsburg vainglorious and haughty Governor Dunmore wanted to expand the territory of Virginia in order to make his domain an endless one. This attitude threw Virginia and Pennsylvania backwoodsmen into conflict, and for a time there was such a strong feeling among the settlers of each colony that it seemed a civil war would be fought over the boundary line.

Traders who depended upon the Indian hunters and trappers to supply them with furs were antagonistic to the settlers. They knew that once a settlement was made, the region was ruined as a trading center. The Indians northwest of the Ohio were aroused. Like the traders, they could see the end of their hunting lands in the wisps of smoke which curled upward from the settler's cabins.

Land gave Simon the same sense of freedom as it did the traders and Indians. But land to speculators and settlers offered another kind of security, a security closely tied up with human society and economics, neither of which Simon understood. Land was at the bottom of every dispute. From the most unscrupulous speculator in Philadelphia and Williamsburg to the poorest settler on the frontier, everyone wished to claim a large fertile block of the Ohio Valley country for himself. The Indian, on the other hand, wanted to keep the virgin land as hunting ground. He considered it his by right of original possession.

Back of this famous border dispute was another long chapter of the white man in North America. Along the seaboard the Englishman who came to the early settlements dreamed that someday he would have a large landed estate. He would bring a wife from England, and they would have sons and daughters who would add glory to his name. These early Englishmen would set up an English society in America. Great fields should be cleared for their crops, and the trees would be deadened on hundreds of acres of rolling pasture land for their livestock.

The Indians were regarded as brutal savages by these early settlers along the seaboard, and they refused to associate with the natives. Few Englishmen or other northern Europeans married Indian women. English ministers of the gospel were not especially adept at converting the Indian to their religion. Instead of being made a part of the new society, he was swept back. All up and down the Atlantic coast the Indian was forced to retreat in the face of an advancing white settlement of his land.

Englishmen came to settle, but the Spaniards and Frenchmen dreamed of making quick fortunes which they would spend in Europe. They came west to trap and trade in furs with the Indians. They took Indian wives and had children. They lived with the Indians in their villages and learned their language and customs and attended all their celebrations. Their priests came among the natives and converted them.

In the end it was an easy matter for these adventurers to slip away from America and leave Indian wives behind. They left the woods as they had found them, and nearly always the Indians remained in a friendly state of mind.

These different attitudes of the white men were to make an important difference in the minds of the Indians. When the English and German pioneers moved westward with their wives, daughters, milch cows, corn patches, and pole cabins, they soon found themselves in conflict with the Indians. From the beginning there was an active dispute which flared up with burning fury every time the whites claimed a large slice of the western country within a short period of time.

This was so in 1773-1774 in the Ohio Valley. Settlement was moving fast. The process was like that of a huge boulder bounding down a mountainside. Every whirl caused it to roll faster. Each year the white population grew larger, and the frontier movement was speeded up. In this rapid advance of settlers many wrongs were committed by both the white man and the Indian.

Virginians and Pennsylvanians quarreled among themselves. The colonial officials were engaged in bitter disputes. Settlers were annoyed by dishonest traders. Bands of hotheaded whites offended Indians, and Indian outlaws offended backwoodsmen.

Each single unfortunate incident touched off a bloody border war. In the frontier cabins were many white men who lacked principle and stability enough to keep them from committing crimes against the Indians. Always in American frontier history there were cowardly troublmakers who had either escaped confinement in the jailhouses or had run off to the woods to practice their meanness.

Even some of the frontier officials lacked honesty and good

judgment, and for selfish reasons they committed mean acts. Among the pioneers in the Ohio Valley was Captain John Conolly, an unscrupulous, hotheaded lieutenant of Governor Dunmore. He was an ill-tempered man who stirred up trouble between the whites and the Indians. In such strife he perhaps thought he saw an opportunity to lead an army of frontiersmen against the natives and to secure glory for himself.

The settler's fear of Indians was constant. He knew only too well the horrors of the surprise raid. Time and again a party of young braves had sneaked through the woods with their faces covered in terrifying white and black stripes of war paint to fire on a lonely cabin.

There were dozens of frontier stories of men murdered and scalped when they were caught off alone in the fields and of women and children captured and taken beyond the Ohio to be tortured to death. Most of these raiding parties had sought horses and plunder. The Indian was tremendously fond of the white man's mount. Raiding parties were known to go hundreds of miles through the unbroken wilderness to steal horses. Conolly played upon these crimes.

Virginians were quickly put into a violent state of mind. Already they believed steadfastly that there was no such thing as a good live Indian. They regarded him as a varmint, and there were few cases where the white man looked upon the killing of an Indian as murder. Failure to regard the Indian as a human being often led to some horrible atrocities on the part of the white frontiersmen.

The Indian looked upon the white man in the same light. Settlers with their accurate long-barreled rifles and their razor-sharp hunting knives and swords were ferocious beings. The Indian believed the enraged white man was a fiercer beast than was the worst savage. Warriors on too many occasions had seen evidence of this when white men had drawn their knives and scalped a fallen brave. To start a war Captain Conolly had only to stir up one bit of trouble.

On April 16, 1774, a small band of hostile Cherokees attacked a white hunting party. They killed one man, wounded another, and robbed the party of its furs. Quickly a letter was sent through the settlement telling everybody to be ready for trouble.

The letter was an excellent excuse. Frontiersmen never waited in the face of what they believed to be a declaration of war. Rifles came down from the buckhorn racks. Knives were sharpened. Everybody was certain the time had come to fight. Angry knots of "Long Knives" met about council fires and pounded the war club on the ground in voting for war.

Among the settlers was a leader named Michael Cresap, born, like Simon, of Irish parents. He had come from Maryland and possessed both faults and virtues. When his temper was aroused, he threw reason and morals to the wind. While he and his neighbors were beating their war clubs angrily before their council fire, a party of hunters was fired upon and robbed near Wheeling. It was a fight between cheating traders and some of their wronged customers.

A trader named Butler (no kin to Simon's "cousin") sent two friendly Shawnees to rescue some of the furs. At Captina, the impulsive Captain Cresap and his comrades overtook the two Indians and murdered them as a matter of principle. When Cresap returned to the camp and was questioned about the Indians, he replied that they had accidentally fallen overboard into the river.

Bullet holes and large smears of fresh blood on the canoes told the truth. The guilty mob had not only killed the braves but had scalped them. After this atrocity Cresap moved rapidly to commit another. He led a party, which included George Rogers Clark, downstream to attack peaceful Shawnees encamped near Grave Creek. This second assault was a base, cowardly act. Cresap and his company had made camp and pretended friendship for the Indians. At a moment when they were least on guard, Cresap's band fell upon them, killing and wounding several. When the whites returned to Wheeling the next day, scalps were displayed as trophies of the fight.

The frontiersmen were now so aroused that there was danger they would stop at nothing. They would commit an act that would take the colony of Virginia into a border war. No Indian was safe from these attacks.

Cresap started on a third expedition of murder against a village of friendly Indians. This group had never been known to mistreat a white man, but they were to be wiped out. The journey through the woods was a long one. Cresap's men had time to think the matter over and to allow their tempers to cool. The village to which they were going was composed largely of women and children. To attack it without a good excuse was nothing short of cowardice. Even a band of men who hated Indians as much as did Cresap's could not go through with such wanton butchery. Perhaps the sobering influence of George Rogers Clark had much to do with this decision. Certainly young Clark possessed more principle than had prompted Cresap's expedition.

One awful tragedy led to another. Indian raiders inflicted crimes upon white settlers, and the settlers paid them back. There was no way short of war to stop these border crimes. Every fiend on the frontier, Indian and white, was out to commit murder.

For years woodsmen and settlers knew the friendly Mingo chief Logan. He was an unusual Indian. When the French had persuaded the Mingoes to make war against the Virginians, Logan had refused to take part in the struggle. He had a great love for the white settlers and for their society. He had learned to speak English more fluently than many of the backwoodsmen. The only crime he ever committed was that of being an Indian.

When Michael Cresap had started his war, Logan and his family were placed in danger. There was at Wheeling another outlaw name Daniel Greathouse—an even greater coward than Michael Cresap.

Greathouse stooped to heartless trickery to bring about the murder of Logan's innocent family. He instructed his agent Baker to sell the Indians all the rum they would drink; when they were drunk, he would get rid of them. He gathered around him thirty-two men and planned to attack the Indians across the river. There were indications, however, that the Indian force was large and that the whites would be defeated.

Greathouse undertook to spy upon the Indian camp and find out how many warriors there really were. Acting the part of a friend, he crossed the river to visit the camp and count the Indians. A friendly squaw begged him to go back. She told him that the Indians were drinking, and that they would kill him. He quickly retreated.

Members of Logan's family and the friendly squaw who had saved Greathouse went to Baker's house on Yellow Creek, where they had always gone for liquor. Baker got them drunk, and then Greathouse and his murderous band killed all of them except one little girl.

Logan was infuriated and swore vengeance upon the white man. He led a band of Mingoes against his former white neighbors and friends. In his first raid he returned with thirteen scalps tied to his belt. The Indians raided and pillaged white cabins, and many of their prisoners were taken across the river to be sacrificed before the warriors' councils. Logan saved one or two of his prisoners and had them adopted into the tribe to replace warriors killed by the Virginians. One of the prisoners was commanded to make gunpowder ink and write a note to Cresap for him. It was a bitter note which contained all the Indian's hatred of the white man:

Captain Cresap:
What did you kill my people of Yellow Creek for? The white people kill my kin at Conestoga, a great while ago, and I thought nothing of that. But you killed my kin again on Yellow Creek, and took my cousin prisoner. Then I thought I must kill too; and I have been three times to war since; but the Indians are not angry; only myself.
Captain John Logan.

Chief Logan tied this message to a war club and left it in a cabin where he had murdered an entire family.

Captain John Conolly had helped to start a fight which frightened him from the beginning. Instead of winning great personal glory, he reaped much anxiety. He took Michael Cresap's command away from him, but Governor Dunmore restored it. A border war was now certain, and the frontiersmen were anxious to get into the fight. Events had happened fast. In the woods along the Kanawha Indians were numerous, and they were in an unhappy frame of mind.

Meanwhile, Simon Kenton discovered that he and his companions were no longer safe in their hunting ground, and they turned back to Fort Pitt. A short time after their arrival in the spring of 1774 the Muskingum War occurred. Kenton's reputation as a woodsman was known, and he was pressed into immediate service along with Jacob Drennon as one of the scouts for Colonel Angus McDonald's expedition to the Muskingum Valley.

Colonel McDonald was a comic-opera commander who bustled about among his men swearing and shaking his sword at them. He had never fought Indians before. The frontiersmen proceeded to ignore his orders and to do unsoldierlike things to the busybodied old Scotchman. Every man came equipped with a tomahawk, a knife, and a gun, and he had seven days' rations strapped to his back. On the trail the old colonel tried to get his men to march in single file in parallel lines. When his highly individualistic men refused to obey his orders, he drew his sword and swore at them. A young boy threatened to use his rifle barrel on the commander and he backed away. The men began to laugh and sing, "The boy scared the colonel."

This army was assaulted by the Indians on a creek bank, but the attackers were driven back. Two white men marching in single file were knocked down with a single bullet. The man in front was killed, and the man behind was wounded. The bullet was pulled out of the second man by a pocket which had been forced into the wound. Colonel McDonald hid behind a log out of the range of fire.

A brave frontier leader was supposed to stand out in front and wave his men on. If he did not, they looked upon him as a coward. McDonald's troops chided him by singing, "Who got behind the log?" and a chorus would answer, "The colonel! the colonel!"

At nightfall the Indians sent messengers to request a council of peace. They asked that two white men be sent as hostages, but no one volunteered. Two Indians came to spend the night in Colonel McDonald's tent to prove their good faith. The scouts knew this was a treacherous ruse, and when Colonel McDonald was asleep, Michael Cresap led most of the troops out of camp for an attack upon the enemy. The surprise attack was the direct result of good scouting on the part of Kenton and Drennon. Cresap's night assault ended the short war. The frontiersmen went back across the river to Fort Pitt. Simon Kenton had his first experience as a spy out ahead of a border army. The slight success of McDonald's comic campaign was due largely to Simon's ability as a woodsman.

At Fort Pitt it was an accepted fact that an Indian war would occur. The little garrison was prepared for a campaign across the river. Woods scouts were called in and kept in readiness to take to the trails ahead of the army.

While waiting for the war to begin, Simon spent his idle time talking with other woodsmen. Already he was an expert, and he enjoyed lying around the fort exchanging yarns of the woods with his fellow scouts. His experiences of the last three years were perhaps more thrilling than those of any other man present. Kenton had come to know intimately the ways of the woods, and the habits of the Indians were no longer mysterious to him.

Among the scouts at Fort Pitt he found many friends whom he remembered throughout his life. For the first time he met George Rogers Clark—a young Virginian of twenty-one who had come west as an adventurer and surveyor. He had roamed through the country along the east bank of the Ohio and had actually gone so far as to build a cabin and to plant the usual patch of corn.

George Rogers Clark was a cocky redheaded young fellow. He knew what he wanted and how to get it. Simon was attracted to him at once. Here was a woodsman who was unafraid and who would stick to his friends in the face of danger. When the scouts sat about the campfire at night, Clark directed talk to the subject of trails. He was a master at getting information.

Simon found it a pleasure to describe his own exploits in the woods to his new friend. He liked Clark's friendly attitude and determination. Also, Clark had spent much time in the western Virginia country, and because of this, the two young men had much in common.

Clark knew little about Indians. He asked Simon, "How do they make their attack? Do they sneak up on you, or do they come in a mad howling mob?" Likewise, he was curious about the Indian's aim. "Can he shoot a rifle as accurately as the white frontiersmen, or does he just point his rifle in the general direction of the enemy and pull the trigger?"

Kenton was able to answer his friend's questions. "The sneaking rascals strike you when you are least expecting them. Just when you get tucked into your robes at night they fire on you. Sometimes they shoot you from behind trees, but lucky for us their aim is poor. When I was off in the woods with old Colonel McDonald's army, our riflemen riddled the red devils. The Shawnees and Wyandottes didn't seem to know how to handle a rifle," said Simon with a chuckle.

Simon liked Michael Cresap. He knew about the Grave Creek murders, but he forgave the big Irishman these crimes, which had occurred in a frontier war. Michael had struck a heavy blow at the Indians and that was the thing which counted most. He was a good natured man and a fine woodsman, who could be depended upon to bring in first-rate information.

Most interesting of all to Simon, however, was a short, swarthy, black-haired and black-eyed youngster named Simon Girty. This boy had the appearance of an Indian dreamer. He seemed more Indian than white and had never known anything but the woods. Simon's own experiences along the Ohio River aroused a feeling of kinship for the boy. He saw in him a likeness of his beloved George Yeager.

Girty was a likable boy, and Simon enjoyed strolling into the woods with him to hear his tales of the borderland. They would sit for hours in a shady nook while he told Kenton of the rich canelands down the river. And he had yarns of buffalo, elk, and bear. There were broad trails through the tall cane, and Girty had sat about the licks watching the game congregate.

Not only was it one of the finest adventure stories Kenton had ever heard, but a valuable lesson in frontier life. Girty's people were Irish. They had come to Pennsylvania as poor immigrants seeking new fortunes on the frontier. But fortune was elusive. Old man Girty was a drunkard who had abused his wife and four sons. The mother helped kill him and ran away with another man.

At the time of Braddock's famous march, the boys were taken prisoners by the Indians at Little Cove. James was taken away by the Shawnees, and George had gone with the Delawares. Simon was made captive by the more peaceable Senecas, and for many years he lived with them. Like Yeager, he had seen much of the frontier country and learned the Indians' mode of life in the forest.

Lying flat on his back and listening to the sorrowful tale of the swarthy backwoodsman, Simon felt great sympathy for the boy. When Girty's cheeks would be flushed and tears rolled down them in the midst of a story about his no-good father or of his trifling mother's neglect of her children, Kenton was deeply touched. After one of these intimate talks, Kenton and Girty clasped hands and swore eternal friendship and fidelity. Simon felt a protective affection for Girty which remained with him always. Girty had told of his ambition to be captain of a militia company and to make of himself a good citizen.

CHAPTER 10

Dunmore's War

When Dunmore's War started, there were two divisions of the Virginia army. Governor Dunmore assumed personal command of the colonial militia of fifteen hundred men and marched it to the head of the Ohio. In southwestern Virginia General Andrew Lewis was instructed to gather his troops from the settlements and hurry with them through the woods to the mouth of the Kanawha.

A call for men went from cabin to cabin. Frontier muster grounds were quickly milling with determined men on their way to join General Lewis's fighting force. James Robertson raised a command, and his rollicking partner John Sevier helped to complete the details of the company. Old Captain Evan Shelby, a stouthearted Marylander, came with a company and brought his young son Isaac, who was getting his first taste of border warfare.

Colonel William Fleming gathered a company and seven captains. Colonel Charles Lewis brought eight captains with his force, and gruff Colonel William Christian had five captains. Here, assembling on the level lands of the Greenbrier, was a patriot's army of the first order, but not a man among the companies was a professional soldier, nor did a single individual represent the crown. Governor Dunmore in a review of it would have seen little to make him proud. The men came dressed like those who had fought twenty years before with Washington in Braddock's army. Every man brought his own long-barreled gun, long knife, tomahawk, and knapsack.

These troops knew nothing about group fighting, and the officers were not interested in their acquiring this knowledge, but their eyes were keen, and they were familiar with the art of moving through the woods. The flickering of the tip of a feather above a log or the sudden appearance of a painted face between the low forks of a tree would be quickly sighted. They were marksmen of the first order. An ordinary rifleman could draw a bead on a cob and pith it at fifty paces. Lovingly, they caressed their guns and called them "Old Betsy," "Thunderation," "Beelzebub" or "Old Jim Ticklers."

These frontiersmen knew nothing about military discipline beyond the old backwoods cry "Every man to his tree." They selected their own officers and followed them into battle out of affection and respect. At the moment of Dunmore's War they were bound together by a common hatred of the Indian, and a few years later they would be united against England.

There was little understanding between Lord Dunmore and General Lewis. When the governor reached Fort Pitt, he changed his plans and decided to go down the Ohio to the Hockhocking and to Pickaway Plains near the famous Indian village of Chillicothe.

Simon Kenton, George Rogers Clark, Simon Girty, and Michael Cresap were sent ahead to scout the woods. This jaunt took Simon over most of the ground he had covered on McDonald's short campaign.

He had become fond of the rugged Ohio country, which gradually leveled out beyond the river hills into large flat bottoms. Privately Simon thought that if his adventure in the woods with Clark, Girty, and Cresap was war, then he loved war.

Once across the Ohio River, Dunmore's army was fairly safe from attack by the Indians. Under the leadership of the stern and unrelenting Chief Cornstalk, the braves had crossed the river to meet General Lewis's army. Governor Dunmore had planned to fight the enemy on his home ground and to destroy his villages. He sent messages back to Girty and a scout named McCullough telling Lewis to move westward, but the general ignored them. Again Dunmore sent the two messengers, and Kenton also.

The Indian lines were drawn tight around the backwoods army at the Kanawha and to get through was a difficult business. Fall had come and the leaves lay deep upon the ground. The nights were brisk with frost, and the early morning along the river brought heavy fog. The scouts picked their way through the woods with extreme caution. The snapping of a single twig would bring a hail of bullets and savage scalping knives. As they got nearer General Lewis's headquarters, there was danger that they would be mistaken for Indians by the quickshooting pickets.

Late one October afternoon Simon and his companions got safely within the militia lines and that night they again slipped into the woods and back through the savage line.

The message commanding General Lewis to move westward to join the governor made the old officer mad. He knew as much as Governor Dunmore about fighting Indians. To move was foolhardy because the woods around him were filled with Cornstalk's braves. Before the sun was up next day, Cornstalk attacked the Virginians. The Indians made powerful thrusts against General Lewis's lines, but each time they were thrown back. The battle was stubborn and bloody. Many frontier officers lost their lives. Victory remained uncertain at nightfall, but in the night the Indians withdrew, giving the victory to the rough Long Knives of the border. Cornstalk's spirit was completely broken. His head was bowed in grief, but the proud old Indian tried to get his men to return to the battle the next day. His brother chiefs refused to fight. There was nothing left but to meet in council and make peace.

Cornstalk's fellow chiefs made it clear that they were sick of fighting and stood ready to make peace with Governor Dunmore. Among the Indians was a white man whom they sent forward with a white flag to ask that the governor appoint an agent who could speak the Indian tongue to arrange the terms of a treaty.

John Gibson, a bright frontiersman, was dispatched to confer with the council of chiefs and discuss the terms of peace. He found Cornstalk in a surly mood, but the other chiefs were in favor of ending the war. Present to talk with Gibson was the grief-stricken Logan—the storm center of the war. Logan took Gibson aside, and with tears streaming down his wrinkled brown cheeks, he repeated the story of the murder of his family. He refused to attend the council with Governor Dunmore and his agents, but he dictated a message for Gibson to take to them.

When Gibson finished reading Logan's brilliant speech, the rough frontiersmen were deeply moved. Even those men who were most bitter in their hatred of the Indians had tears in their eyes.

Logan accused Cresap of killing his family. George Rogers Clark jeered the headstrong captain. "I knew you were wrong, Michael," said Clark. "Now the chief has found you out, and someday he will smoke your hide at the stake."

Nearby sat the cowardly William Greathouse. The very sight of the rascal infuriated Cresap, and he drew his knife and threatened to scalp him.

Simon knew all the details of the Logan murder and was

sorry for the grieving Indian. He left the council and went to see Chief Logan. Quickly the two became fast friends. In their conversation Kenton looked upon Logan as a badly wronged man who deserved the white man's friendship.

When the peace treaty was made, Simon Kenton was free to take up his hunting where he had left off the spring before. Girty had refired his ambition to see the Kentucky caneland, and he began making preparations to visit it.

On every hand militiamen were packing up and saying good-bye. They were ready to set out for their cabins in the settlements and to take home with them the happy news that the border was at last safe from the Indians.

Below Fort Pitt at Point Pleasant, General Lewis's buckskin army was already in the mountains. Captain Shelby and his son Isaac were on their way to a reunion with their families. General Lewis went home a sorrowful man. He had lost his brother Charles in the battle.

At Fort Pitt, Captain Conolly was relieved at the ending of the war he had helped to start. Both Dunmore and the Tory-minded Conolly realized that this war had been a serious mistake. It had injured the cause of the crown by helping to unite the frontiersmen in a common group, and Dunmore's treaty with the Indians had in reality extended the frontiersman's claim to the land beyond the Ohio. There was to be, he hated to admit to himself, a free America.

Simon Kenton saw the backwoods movement for freedom begin at the mouth of the Hockhocking River. A group of frontier officers and soldiers met in council and adopted rousing resolutions of good wishes for the delegates meeting in the Continental Congress in Philadelphia.

It was a proud moment for Simon. He was twenty years of age and twice already had been an advance guard before frontier armies. These armies wrote one important chapter in American history, and he was a part of it.

Simon, like all of the other woodsmen, knew that the day would come when cabins and cornfields and cow pastures would exist where now there was forest. His young mind was filled with many conflicting thoughts of things that had happened and of things his comrades said were to be.

When the rugged Virginia troops rode away waving their long, clumsy rifles high over their heads and shouting rollicking farewells to the settlers at Fort Pitt, Simon was again homesick. These soldiers were going home, a privilege denied to him. But as the last echo of the departing, boisterous soldiers spent itself in the valley, he remembered the fabulous caneland of Kentucky.

Simon Girty's story had pleased Simon. Perhaps back in 1771, when they were drifting southward, he had doubted that such a land as Kentucky existed, except in Yeager's imagination. Perhaps he had thought, as they tugged at the canoe going upstream, that Yeager was too enthusiastic and his tale a thing

born of a childish imagination, but Girty gave him assurance
that Yeager's story was true. He would put off into the great
woods again, but he needed a dependable companion, a canoe,
and a store of hunting supplies. Then he would go once more
in search of Kentucky. This time he meant to succeed.

Simon searched for a single companion. Two men could
make decisions quickly. His experience with Yeager and Strader
had taught him that it was much easier for two men to escape
an Indian raid than when there were more. Also, there was far
less danger of a quarrel. He chose Thomas Williams, a congenial
fellow who had all the characteristics of a good woodsman.
Simon had known Williams in Dunmore's War, and he was
certain they could live together in peace on a long hunt.

In late summer 1776, they shoved their heavy canoe into
the Ohio and set out for the Kentucky country. This was Simon's
fourth journey in search of the great hunting ground. As the
canoe glided out of sight of the fort, and the scattered settlers'
cabins began to appear on the left bank of the river, Simon's
mind was troubled. There were certain well known landmarks
he could identify at a glance, but there were thousands of hidden
marks which he neither knew nor could find.

It was difficult to keep track of the mileage. The wide Ohio
River, threading its way around hundreds of sharp bends, was
a confusing stream. Island points and shoulders of land jutted
into the stream. The trees grew down to the water's edge in
a widespreading roll of foliage, and matted branches obscured
the lay of the land to a man in a canoe.

At LeTart's Falls a French trader described to Simon and
William in detail the appearance of the tall limestone bank
opposite the caneland. At the upper end was the mouth of Cabin
Creek, and a short way downstream was the mouth of Limestone Creek. The Ohio went westward and then turned directly
southwestward around a sharp bend. For several miles the river

straightened out. A shelf of heavily wooded ground tapered down to its edge. Standing as a backdrop to this natural landing place was the huge elbow which dug its way deep back into the curving Ohio Bluff. The trader's description was clear, and Simon was convinced that he recalled having seen the place four years before.

Once they were back in their canoe, however, the confusing spell of the Ohio was again upon Simon. Midway of every stretch of land, around every abrupt bend of the river, he thought he saw the place described by the trader. Many times on this trip the two boatmen pulled their canoe to shore only to find that Simon's imagination was tricking him. Soon, like Yeager, Kenton lost all sense of distance, and every rising shelf of land south of the Ohio became a nightmare.

Winter was coming on and the two men were uncertain of the land and its hunting possibilities. Simon turned back to the Big Sandy where he had a hunted a year before. Here they built a winter camp and awaited the coming of spring to go in search of Kentucky. It was the fourth winter Simon Kenton had set a trap line between the Big Sandy and the Kanawha. This country had almost become his homeland.

At every place where silt eddied at the stream edges, there were the paths of fur-bearing animals which hunted and fished for food along the river and through the woods. There were mink, otter, beaver, raccoon, and foxes.

Here was fur enough to make a trapping party rich. Soon Simon's traps, deadfalls, and pits were yielding a prosperous return in skins. Day by day the improvised fur bin at the hunting camp was being stocked with precious skins which would go to buy supplies in the spring. Simon's rifle brought down a bountiful supply of meat, and his skinning knife was kept busy preparing hoops for stretching skins and trimming away bits of fat from the hides.

For Simon this winter's hunting had a purpose. It was a key to his future happiness. Every skin stacked carefully away in his cache was in reality a step nearer the Kentucky dreamland. He had searched for this land so long that it had become an insatiable passion with him. Dragging his weary body into his hard bed inside the lean-to, Simon pulled his skin robes up under his chin and lay awake for hours dreaming of the spring's adventures.

When the leaves were out again and the dogwood and redbud were splotching the green woodlands with their burst of blooms, he and Williams passed down the Big Sandy into the Ohio and awaited the arrival of an Indian trader. From him they would secure a new stock of supplies and then again go in search of Kentucky. This time Simon knew they would not fail. He was getting a head start, and winter could not drive him to cover as it had before.

Fortune was with them. On the Ohio they met the same French trader who had described Limestone Creek and its landmarks to them. Again Simon had the trader go over all the details so that he would be certain not to go astray. Simon was impatient in the exchange of furs and hides for supplies. The stowing of each parcel seemed an endless task, but finally they pushed the canoe away with its precious load of corn, meal, salt, and hunting materials.

Again the confusion of the river caused uncertainty. A chance landing brought Simon's canoe upon a long bar where a nearby creek tumbled down to the river. A short distance away the bluff towered over them like a huge bowed wall. A careful examination revealed that this was the place for which they were searching.

Every tree, the creek, every ridge and point of land fitted in perfectly with the descriptions of Yeager and the Frenchman. It was like working for days at a time upon a complicated puzzle and then suddenly having every piece fall into place almost of its own accord.

In a moment of triumph Simon stood and gazed at the great elbow of bluff folding back away from him. The sun peeped over it, and long shadows were falling far out on the Ohio. Ordinarily he would have been busy making camp, but Simon was too happy to be concerned with this chore. Beyond the bluff was cane, and for miles beyond was Kentucky country. Here was the spot for which Yeager had searched so diligently.

CHAPTER 11

Caneland

Simon's impatience to be up and over the high bluff was that of a child. He did not want the sun to set on another day without his having seen Kentucky. While Thomas Williams worked to unload the canoe and make camp, Simon climbed the long hill by way of the game trail. As the sun dropped slowly into the hazy timberline to his right, Simon stood gazing in a fit of intoxication at the cane-covered ridges before him.

Never before in all his life had he been so happy as at the moment he stood there watching the rays of the setting sun play upon the weaving trim cane. Not far away a young deer bleated. Simon shot it and returned to camp to celebrate his good fortune by having the finest of all frontier treats—broiled hams of deer.

Beyond the limestone bluff the next morning Kenton and Williams found great stretches of fertile land. A wide game trail led southward, and the two hunters made their way to a spot well beyond the crest of the bluff before they rested their burden of supplies on the ground.

The land was rolling. Long, gentle ridges tumbled down to the broad, shallow valleys, and then rolled in long waves to new peaks. Soil in this place was a far cry from the red hillsides which Mark Kenton cultivated in Fauquier County. Here a man could run his toe through the rich brown loam and turn it up to the sun. Back home in Virginia Simon had heard old-timers say "land was as rich as a bed of ashes." This described perfectly the fine Kentucky caneland.

All about were signs that there was game aplenty. Deep trails had been made by elk, deer, and buffalo. Occasionally there was a dark tunnel where a waddling fat bear had burrowed his way through the matted undergrowth. Not far away a vain gobbler brushed his stiff wing feathers over hard brown shins and paid court to a crowd of clucking hens.

Simon knew at once that this was the place he wanted to pitch his camp and begin explorations. Four miles back from the Ohio, well over the rim of the great bluff, he and Williams cut and burned the cane from an acre of ground and with their tomahawks dug hills and dropped seed corn, which they had bought from the trader. Then they built a pole cabin and moved into it.

The two men mixed hunting with watching a corn crop. By the time the corn was in hard roasting ear, they had gained much useful knowledge of that part of Kentucky. As fall came on, they broadened their circle. South of them was the great crossroads of the game trails, the Lower Blue Lick.

The Licking River doubled back on itself in a sharp double curve. Crowded down deep in the upper side of one of these elbows was a long barren ridge heavily strewn with thin pieces of rotten lime and sandstone. Its rocky side was stripped bare of foliage, and it had the appearance of being a vast wilderness cowpen. A horde of milling feet had worn the surface bare.

Where the ridge sloped down to a point in the river bend, there was a huge natural panbowl where many springs poured out flush rivulets of salty blue water. In the middle of this bowl for a space of two acres was a sticky mire stirred day after day by the thirsty grazing animals who licked the savory mud for salt. Never had Simon beheld a wonder of this sort. At one place on the wide trail he stopped to watch the endless stream of buffalo pass by. He counted fifteen hundred in a single herd.

Simon killed a buffalo, and they had huge roasted steaks fresh from the coals of their campfire. That night, there on the bank of the Licking River, Simon rolled himself in his skin blanket and made his body comfortable on the ground before the blazing log heap. He dreamed of the endless paradise into which he had wandered. He would spend the winter exploring the country. Curiosity tempted him to follow the trails southward to see where they would lead.

The next morning Simon and Williams went to the lick to watch droves of animals milling about. Down the trail came two white men. Simon was surprised to see men of his own color and tongue coming toward him. Since he and Williams had left the French trader early in the spring, he had seen only one other human being—an Indian with whom he had suddenly found himself face to face on a sharp bluff of the Licking country. Both had been surprised. Neither man had the advantage of the other, and it was a moment that required diplomacy. The Indian offered Simon a handful of gunpowder as a token of friendship and then went on his way.

The two white men coming down the trail explained to Kenton and Williams that they had lost their canoe and were stranded in the wilderness without guns and supplies. Their names were Hendricks and Fitzpatrick, and they were trying to cut across country to the settlements east of the mountains.

Fitzpatrick was impatient to be on his way. Simon begged him to stay on in the wilderness. "Stay with us, Fitzpatrick, and we will have a fine year of hunting. It's too far from here to Virginia for one man to make the journey."

But Fitzpatrick was stubborn. "I'm going back to the settlements or die trying. I'm sick of these woods. They crowd in upon me. This is a terrible place to live," he told Kenton and Williams.

Hendricks was not so anxious to leave Kentucky once they had found Simon and his companion. He begged the woodsmen to go back to the Ohio with his anxious comrade, and he would remain behind and rest until they returned.

On the way to the Ohio, the three woodsmen stopped by Kenton's cabin to equip Fitzpatrick for his long journey upstream. They gave him a bag of parched corn, a gun, a handful of gunpowder, and some shot. Likewise, they gave him a buffalo robe and some new moccasins and sent him on his way.

When Fitzpatrick had gone, Simon and Williams returned to their camp to join Hendricks. They looked forward to hunting with him. Fall was in the air, and Simon had seen a few signs of Indian hunters. He told Williams, "Yesterday I came on a fresh killed buffalo carcass which the Shawnees left behind. We are going to have to be careful with the Indians hunting in the woods." Suddenly he remembered that Hendricks was alone. "I hope," said Kenton, "that our new friend is safe. I am afraid he isn't familiar enough with the western woods to protect himself."

Simon was suddenly frightened at what might have happened to the lone white man near the Blue Lick. He speeded up his own pace and urged Williams on. After a day of travel, the pair was at the foot of the hill that lay between them and the camp. Ahead of them, a thin wisp of smoke worked its way up through the trees in a spiral. All about were Indian signs. There was an acrid smell in the air.

Closer to the camp, Simon discovered it had been raided. Hendricks was not in sight, and it would be too much of a chance for them to go straight to the fire. For the rest of the day they lay in hiding.

Across the ridge from them was a large party of warriors who spent the day torturing Hendricks at the stake. The next morning Simon and Williams found his bones and seared bits of flesh smoldering in the deserted campfire. Simon realized they had been unforgivably careless. Perhaps they could have saved Hendricks by more positive action.

Hendricks's death was a horrible tragedy. Simon was inconsolable as he and Williams covered the campfire with dirt they dug up with an ax. This mishap was a gruesome warning to use a lot more care in the future.

Another hunter surprised Simon at the Blue Lick at a later time. Kenton discovered that someone was hiding near him, and when he yelled for the stranger to step out and make himself known, he was astonished to hear a man ordering him in English to come from behind his tree. James Galloway, a lanky Pennsylvania long hunter, was taking a short cut to the Ohio on his return trip home. Galloway had discovered Kenton, and for some time he thought he was watching an Indian. Perhaps for a moment Simon was in grave danger of being shot. He had sat out in the open bareheaded like an Indian working with his rifle. Like Daniel Boone, during his long stay in the wilderness, Simon supposed there were no other persons around, and he lived in the woods as if he and Williams were alone.

One day shortly before getting started southward, Simon discovered a white hunter standing on the opposite side of the panbowl. The man before him, he soon learned, was a famous frontier scout—Michael Stoner, a jovial and stocky man of the frontier. He was a bosom friend of Boone and had watched the rapid changes going on in Kentucky.

Stoner told Simon that already settlers were moving into Kentucky. Daniel Boone had built a fort south of the Kentucky River; a short way downstream a company of Virginians, under the leardership of James Harrod, were living at Harrod's Station;

and on Elkhorn Creek was another station. This was startling news. His journey of exploration would now have a new significance. No longer was Kentucky only an inviting caneland where game existed in plenty.

Every day new settlers were pushing through the woods from Cumberland Gap to the stations. Others were drifting down the Ohio and up the Kentucky to the new settlements. The Kentucky country was becoming civilized. Simon felt that he was in the midst of an unhappy dream. He had planned all summer to spend the fall and winter hunting deeper into the Kentucky country. He had looked forward to a winter of wandering in the tall cane and of running trap lines along the streams without molestation from other human beings.

The story sounded so unreasonable that Simon doubted its authenticity. For four years he had been too much interested in hunting, exploring, and Indian fighting to pay much attention to what was going on around him. Almost under his nose surveyors and land scouts were pouring southward down the Ohio River to the Kentucky country. A dozen canoes loaded with land agents and their helpers had swung around in the wide eddy caused by the mouth of the Kentucky and had gone up that stream looking for good locations in which to plant a settlement.

Simon had even accompanied one such party downstream. Somehow, in his boyish love for the wilderness, he never realized that the men were anything more than hunters like himself. For the first four years he wandered through the great woods without giving serious thought to personal ownership of the land. The woods were free to everybody who wished to hunt in them and that was enough for him.

But while Simon wandered carefree through the Ohio Valley, the frontier line east of the mountains was thrust forward with vigorous force. Determined settlers, their faces westward, were

on the march. Roads and trails leading up and down the great valley of Virginia were crowded with families moving on.

Before Simon and Thomas Williams had reached the mouth of Limestone Creek in May, one important chapter of Kentucky's history was already written. A year before, James Harrod and a party of land hunters had drifted down the Ohio from Pennsylvania to the mouth of the Kentucky.

But at the place where Kenton, Yeager, and Strader had turned back, Harrod's party had gone upstream for seventy miles. When the tall, blue limestone palisades towered highest overhead, Harrod's men deserted their boats and went south of the river for eight or nine miles to scout the land.

On a sprawling green knoll, where a fresh spring of water gushed out of a crack in the limestone, they began a settlement. Harrod's axes bit deep into the young walnut, ash, oak, and cherry. Crashing down with a great thundering, the long-bodied sapplings broke the stillness of virgin Kentucky. One by one the trees were cleared from the ground, and logs were stacked into pyramid-shaped piles alongside of cabin sites. At regular intervals four piles of bleached limestone marked the corners of each new cabin.

Sweating men, clad in tasseled and fringed hunting shirts and doeskin breeches, notched and raised the logs into place.

Square sides of the cabin walls rose high above the ground. The time came when it was a cheering sight for James Harrod's men to stand at one end of the narrow avenue between the cabins and look at the completed walls. As their axes cut away thick slices from the sides of the heavy timbers, and one log was saddled on top of another in close-fitting notches, these men began to dream of a day when a town would exist on that site.

James Harrod and his companions were erecting the first Kentucky settlement. They were planting the foot of the white man firmly in the land beyond the mountains.

Fear of the Indian vanished, until one day two bedraggled white travelers strolled among the cabins. Daniel Boone and his companion, Michael Stoner, were on their 900-mile mission to warn the surveyors at the Falls of the Ohio to return to Virginia.

As Boone stood and sighted down Harrod's cabin walls, he recalled his own blighted ambition to be the first settler in the region. Two years previously he had become enthusiastic about the Kentucky country and persuaded his wife Rebecca and several of their neighbors to cross the mountains with him. A surprise Indian attack near Cumberland Gap had turned his party back to the Holston Valley, postponing settlement in Kentucky until a more favorable day.

News of Dunmore's victory set in progress another movement toward Kentucky from east of the mountains. Judge Richard Henderson of North Carolina had organized a land company with Nathaniel and Thomas Hart, James Hogg, and others as partners. He planned to move west to the fertile land which the romantic Boone had described to him and there found a private empire. He called his company Transylvania; he hoped he could get Daniel Boone to act as his scout.

At Sycamore Shoals in the Watauga River, Judge Henderson and the dignified members of his land company made long and pretty speeches to the Cherokee Indians gathered around the council fire. Their supply of rum cheered the braves as much as their speeches. Hundreds of gaudy trinkets displayed by skillful clerks caught the eyes of the Indians, and soon a treaty of purchase was made.

The Transylvania Land Company came into possession of Boone's paradise. They now controlled that huge strip of free land which Daniel had roamed over during the two years of his long hunting. A trail right through the mountains was purchased from the generous chiefs, and Daniel Boone was sent ahead to locate a path through the woods and to begin a station on the Kentucky River.

Beyond Cumberland Gap, Daniel Boone and his men worked fast. Their task was to find the best and most direct trail possible from Cumberland Gap northward. They blazed trees along the way with long glancing licks of their tomahawks. Low-hanging limbs were cut back, and shallow fording places across the many rivers and creeks clearly marked. Boone moved his men along in a hurry; he was about to realize a long-standing ambition to settle in Kentucky. He resented the fact that limbs and fording places delayed his progress. He could hardly wait until he arrived at the Kentucky to begin felling trees with which to build a cabin.

At the head of his party, Daniel Boone traveled with a positive step. This time the name of Boone would be planted firmly upon Kentucky soil. Although a lover of the woods, he could visualize the day when the sharp command of the settler to his oxen would send the clumsy wooden plow ripping through the heavy turf of the canebrakes. The forest would fall back, and cabin chimneys would send up long spirals of smoke to signal the growth of a Kentucky civilization. Amidst these pleasant daydreams, Daniel Boone's men marked their trail; the blazes were to be permanent. Thousands of weary settlers with packhorses would follow them mile after mile through the bewildering forest to the fertile lands of Transylvania.

Boone pushed his men ahead rapidly to the south bank of the Kentucky. They stood over this stream on a cold March day where the palisades dipped deeply down to the slender green river which marked the Transylvania Company's northern boundary. Somewhere in the neighborhood of this place Boone intended to locate his settlement. During their first night they got a notion of what price they would have to pay for Kentucky. When the Indians attacked, Captain Twetty was shot through both legs and left to die. A black servant was killed, and Felix Walker was wounded so badly that he could not be moved for twelve days. When he was able to stir again, the entries in his journal were changed from a tone of excitement and adventure to one of fear and doubt. Walker was stunned by the rapidity and fierceness with which the Indians struck.

Boone knew that Indian attacks would come. Several times before on his trips he had experienced lightning-like assualts— a hardship which the frontiersman had to accept as a natural course of affairs. Boone's message to Colonel Henderson had a ringing note of enthusiasm. For fear his employer would balk upon hearing the news of the raid, he begged him to come on at once. From the scene of the attack Boone moved upstream to the mouth of Otter Creek. There he began building cabins for the station.

Boone's fort was a long, rectangular log structure with two-story blockhouses rearing their broad shoulders above the puncheon wall at each corner. Along the sides were low cabins with crude roofs slanting inward. Enclosing the spaces between the cabins were tall panels of round log puncheons driven deep into the ground and fastened overhead to strong posts and railings. In the middle of each side wall was swung a wide gate to admit the rapid passage into the fort of both people and livestock. Behind the stout protecting walls of this fort, Daniel Boone and Richard Henderson planted the roots of white society in Simon Kenton's caneland.

Down the Kentucky a short distance, James Harrod and his men returned to their deserted cabins and began work where they had left off the year before. This time Harrod's little group of cabins would have a new meaning. His settlement was to symbolize Virginia's expansion into the Kentucky region.

Down the Wilderness Road from Harrod's settlement, near the head of Dick's River, Benjamin Logan had built a cabin. In the immediate future he planned to expand it into a frontier station. Logan had been a member of Dunmore's army which had gone to Pickaway Plains in 1774. There he had seen Simon Kenton, and in later years he and Simon became intimate friends.

Across the Kentucky on the north fork of Elkhorn Creek another settlement was started in the early fall months. Surveyors explored much of that fertile stretch of land, which sat like a jewel in a massive setting formed by the big bend of the Kentucky River around two sides with the knobs and mountains on the others. Agents of the land barons knew at once that this region would be the center of Kentucky settlement. Here cane grew thickest and game was most plentiful. From almost every hillside, springs sent rivulets of fresh water racing toward shallow creeks. The soil was deep, and where there were open spaces in the cane, emerald-green grass stuck up sharp, slender blades to form a veritable carpet.

Huge post oak, hackberry, walnut, sugar maple, and cherry

trees dotted the land. There was something strange about this region: grass grew right up to the trees and was as virile in the shade as in the sunshine. This had attracted the attention of the early hunter, and now it was a thing that caught the eyes of the land speculator. In this region of deeply matted bluegrass and massive trees, the settlers would grow fine livestock. On every hand trees bore the familiar tomahawk landmarks. The land claimant was already stepping off choice plots of this vast frontier pasture land.

The fall of 1775 found a party of landseekers caught in the region with winter rapidly approaching. Indian hostilities were increasing, and it was necessary for the surveyors to make camp. They went to the huge Royal Spring, which poured out thousands of gallons of water per minute down a wild race, and there located their cabins. Among these men were the McClelland brothers for whom the station was named and the McConnell brothers.

Elsewhere in the Kentucky woods, settlers' cabins were popping up. Rugged individuals who had lived all their lives in isolated cabins were coming down the Ohio or were struggling through Cumberland Gap to take their chances with the Indians. On a branch of the Licking, John Cooper had built a cabin and raised a crop of corn. John Hinkston had built a blockhouse which formed the core for a frontier station.

Almost overnight Kentucky's wilderness was becoming a settled region. Across the Ohio Indians shook their heads around council fires and clenched their fists and gritted their teeth in angry determination to drive the white man back beyond the settlement line east of the mountains. The Indians planned vigorous spring campaigns. They would run from one station to the other. One by one, they would wipe out the white settlements just as they had always destroyed nests of bothersome yellow jackets.

CHAPTER 12

A Kentucky Visit

The year of 1776 was a bloody one in Kentucky. Angry warriors swarmed along the deeply worn trails, swung their heavy clubs, and wrought bitter vengeance upon the droves of white settlers coming over the mountains. Simon Kenton's virgin caneland was undergoing a sudden change.

Simon faced a new and strange future before the end of his first year in the happy hunting ground. His days of free hunting were over. Gradually after his meeting with Stoner, Simon became less a hunter and more an Indian scout for the Kentucky settlers. Michael Stoner's arrival at the Lower Blue Lick with a fabulous story of Kentucky had introduced a change of plan. From the brisk fall morning when the chunky Dutchman stammered through his long tale of the settlements to the south, until the last Indian was driven back across the Ohio in defeat, Simon Kenton was a central figure in the ferocious struggle of the frontier.

Michael Stoner went to the Lawrence Creek cabin with Kenton and Williams to spend the night. There he continued his account of the work of Boone and Harrod and of the long string of immigrants pouring in over the Wilderness Road. The next day he and Simon began a tour of the stations.

To Simon this visit was highly exciting. For four years he had not come under the pleasant influence of civilized families living in cabins. Not since he left the home of his "Cousin" Butler back on the Cheat River had Simon been in touch with a life watched over by women. In his visit along the Kentucky with settlers who had come in overland from North Carolina and Virginia, he got his first glimpse of the civilization that was being firmly planted upon Kentucky soil.

Unlike most woodsmen in American history, Simon was a jovial, talkative soul. Daniel Boone was tight-lipped and had to be drawn out. It was a matter of picking the great woodsman bit by bit to learn anything from him, but Simon was the direct opposite. He sat for hours talking of adventures in the woods. He liked to spin yarns and to joke with the settlers. His stories of his own exploits were modest ones.

With shoulder-shrugging timidity Simon would repeat many of the experiences of his numerous long hunts. Everywhere the settlers liked this friendly young man, not yet turned twenty-one, who seemed to be so sound in his judgment. His forthrightness and obliging nature inspired immediate confidence. Simon was the kind of youth who could accept responsibility and prove faithful to the end. All his life he served his fellows with that good-natured Irish generosity, which ever ignored his own best personal interest.

During this early fall jaunt around the circle of forts, he met old friends and made new ones. There was activity wherever he went. Axes rang in a loud clamor through the forest. Tall trees came crashing down to the ground in the clearings and were cut into long lengths for logs with which to build cabin walls. Huge square timbers were shaped for the walls of the strong corner blockhouses, and long poles were sharpened and drilled for puncheons to be placed in the stockade walls.

On every side men whooped and yelled commands to bony

horses straining at the end of rawhide traces as they "snaked" long logs into place. Before a clumsy hand-hewn block, a pioneer in coonskin cap and skin hunting shirt hammered with a maul upon a frow riving broad, thin boards for cabin rooftops. A man with a long, greasy queue hanging down his back was smoothing a rough split log floor, with a foot adz. Other men rolled long, dripping straw and mud bats with which to build crude stick and dirt chimneys. Women cooked over beds of scorching coals before wide hearths or sat long hours before spinning wheels and clumsy looms making thread and cloth. Girls spent hours walking back and forth to the springs bringing water. They wore hollowed shoulder yokes for balancing two piggins. Children were engaged in watching the cows and sheep, which grazed in the nearby clearings and woods.

Everywhere men were busy settling their families upon the fertile soil of the new country. They were too busy to fool away precious time recording the happenings around them. Thus we do not know when the two famous woodsmen, Kenton and Boone, met for the first time. Perhaps it was without ceremony before the gate at Boonesborough. Boone doubtless greeted Simon in his characteristic clipped manner by simply saying, "Howdy, Butler." There is an old legend that these two men met in the woods. The story does great credit to them as expert woodsmen. It was said that early one morning the two approached a fording place in a northern Kentucky river. They looked up quickly to see each other at the same moment. Both looked so much like Indians that they faded instantly into the woods. All day they maneuvered through the woods, each trying to get the drop on the other. It was a great display of craftiness that the two men kept so well under cover, and it was not until late afternoon that one of them discovered the other was a white man.

At Boonesborough Simon met not only Daniel Boone but

the Callaways, Richard Henderson, and Rebecca Boone. Down the river at Harrod's Town he saw many of his fellow Virginians. There he renewed acquaintance with his fellow scout of Dunmore's War, George Rogers Clark. At the other stations he formed a friendship with Benjamin Logan, the McClellands, the McConnells, and the Todds.

Simon, under his assumed name, felt that he was free from danger of recognition, and his visit was unmarred by this fear. Everywhere he gathered news of the settlements. When he and Williams came away from a lone cabin or a station, he had an accurate knowledge of its location and the people who lived there.

During this journey Simon got to know most of the people in Kentucky, where they came from, and what they brought with them. Simon was a keen historian and news reporter. Like so many men of his time who could neither read nor write, his memory was active, and once he acquired a bit of information, he retained it. He had developed an amazing sense of geography. The maze of Kentucky trails was baffling. Even so good a woodsman as Stoner occasionally lost his way.

At the time Simon and Williams came on him at the Lower Blue Licks, Stoner was exploring the new country to determine the lay of the land. In a sense he was lost because he had never learned the course of the great buffalo trail. For Simon there was never any confusion of routes. A fork or the turning of a trail stamped itself upon his memory. Fords were familiar to him. He had a natural sense of the importance of landmarks, an ability that was to prove of great significance in the campaigns about to begin in Kentucky. Simon came to know the trails so well that when one was blocked, he was always able to locate an alternate route. Long years in the woods had given him a sense of bearing not surpassed at any time by any other woodsman.

Before Simon and Thomas Williams could recross the Licking and return to their cabins and hunting ground on Lawrence Creek and around Blue Licks, Indian pressure was making itself felt along the trails. They were forced to stop at Hinkston's blockhouse for the winter, and Simon became a hunter and scout for the settlement. During the cold winter months he was able to go on with his career as a woodsman. Occasionally a stray warrior crossed his path or a white land hunter would appear suddenly in the woods before him, but on the whole the woods were relatively quiet.

Game was plentiful, and Simon fetched in a bountiful supply of meat. For a long time he had two faithful dog companions. At night in the woods they slept on either side of him, and at the cracking of a twig by a prowling animal or an Indian, they barked a loud alarm. Simon had come to depend upon them as his personal guardians on the long nights spent in the woods. One day he came upon a lone buffalo licking at a frozen claybank. His dogs charged it. Each of them grabbed an ear and when the surprised bull reared up and lunged forward, the dogs held on. The ground was covered with ice, and the buffalo charged down the frozen embankment toward the Licking River. The animal's feet slipped out from under it, and its huge carcass slid down rapidly to the frozen river. When it landed on the solid surface with a heavy impact, the ice broke and both buffalo and dogs went through and were drowned.

At the end of the long winter when the trails were again open to travel, Simon, Williams, and a third companion, Samuel Arrowsmith, returned to Lawrence Creek. They planted a crop of corn and took up their lives in the wilderness where they had left off in the fall. By the end of the first week of April, long immigrant boats were shoving their snubbed prows deep into the soft sandbars at Limestone Creek, and anxious settlers were clamoring up the steep Ohio bluff to seek land claims along the wide game trail. Settlers coming from Fort Pitt had learned that by beaching their boats at Limestone and walking overland to central Kentucky, they could cut off several hundred miles of travel by water. Otherwise they had to round the big hump of Kentucky country and then travel seventy or eighty miles against the stiff current of the Kentucky to land near their destination.

The buffalo road began to take on the appearance of a main thoroughfare in a busy country. Settlers were showing their heads every week above the rim of the bluff. When they arrived at Limestone, they found Kenton on hand either to give them advice or to act as their guide to settlements. Simon always knew where they could find good land and reasonable safety.

During the spring and summer months Simon was everywhere. Immigrants not too familiar with the woods and its dangers found in him a lifesaving source of information and protection. Always Simon was ready to offer his services. He was quick, however, to realize that when a settler piled his goods on the ground at Limestone, he needed most of all an experienced guide. He remembered with heart-sickening horror that slender shaft of nauseating smoke which had drifted up a year before from the smoldering bones of Hendricks, and to atone for what he always considered a lack of caution on his own part, he was anxious to see the newcomers safely to their new homes.

Indians were everywhere. There were numerous signs along the warriors' path; daubs of war paint were fresh. Crude paintings of the war bird appeared on the faces of the flat rocks jutting out from the banks of the streams and along the hillsides. A settler unfamiliar with the woods headed for certain destruction if he undertook to travel alone.

Simon went on many trips southward to lead the newcomers to Hinkston's, McClelland's, Boone's, and Harrod's stations. Among these were the Stocktons, the Virgins, John McCauseland, and William Grayden. One day Simon's old friend Jacob Drennon appeared at Limestone. The two recalled their scouting days around Fort Pitt and in the Muskingum valley.

At the Big Bone Lick Drennon was so entranced with the large number of game animals gathered about the lick that he bribed a Delaware Indian to tell him of another such place. The Delaware described the rugged country around the mouth of the Kentucky, and Jacob slipped away from the party and ran ahead to claim the land around the mineral spring which today bears his name. Simon was happy to have his old friend in Kentucky, and he led him to an excellent location on Lawrence Creek where a fine spring bubbled up out of a hillside. There Drennon established a temporary cabin and corn-patch claim to a piece of land, and in later years he became a neighbor of Kenton's.

While Simon Kenton kept busy in Kentucky piloting settlers

to the stations or locating land claims for them, the Americans east of the mountains were in a turmoil. The thirteen colonies were breaking away from the crown. That summer in Philadelphia another piedmont Virginian—Thomas Jefferson—was drafting a declaration of independence. Kenton's old companions in arms who had fought with Dunmore and Lewis were now preparing for a bigger fight for the freedom of America.

The English quickly made allies of their former Indian enemies. At Detroit Governor Henry Hamilton opened a drive against the Virginia outposts in Kentucky. He stirred vigorously the Indians' wrath against the encroaching white settlers to the south. It was said in Kentucky that he offered bounties for white scalps which the marauding braves fetched back with them from over the Ohio.

All summer the warriors lay in ambush about the frontier cabins and stations, waiting for unsuspecting immigrants to appear along the trails or watching for the unguarded moment when careless pioneers got too far from the protecting walls of their cabins and stations. These attacks started first along the south bank of the Ohio and then reached as far into Kentucky as Cumberland Gap. On the front line of this assualt, Simon was able to know when the Indians would appear. He kept a close watch before the stations, and when a raiding party sneaked over the Ohio under cover of darkness, he shadowed their advance. On many occasions his lithe brown body glided through the woods unseen by the Indians to warn unsuspecting backwoodsmen of their peril. Often he stood before a lone cabin door or at the gate of a fort and pounded with his tomahawk to signal the approach of a raid.

With each passing month of the summer of 1776, the raids grew in intensity. Soon they began to have a telling effect upon the settlements. Inside dingy pole cabins, women and children were frantic with fear. Weaklings among the men began to grumble and to talk of turning back for the older settlements beyond the mountains. Along the trails timid immigrants turned their pack horses around and hastened to safety. Simon enjoyed the excitement of these first months. He had a perfect record. Not a single raiding party got past him.

Nearly every day a scout came in to report the murder and scalping of immigrants traveling through the woods. Several times Simon himself had come upon the scalped and mutilated bodies of luckless human beings caught alone. Occasionally an Indian was captured from whose belt dangled the stained blond locks of a white child or woman. Packs of household goods were found torn to bits and scattered over the woods, the horses having been stolen by the Indians. Life in the wilderness was becoming a grim matter even for a stouthearted woodsman. Only the most experienced frontiersmen on the open trails could keep out of the way of Hamilton's native allies.

About the forts and cabins it was necessary to maintain a constant vigil. Cows in their nearby pens were forever throwing up their heads and watching the woods with nervous apprehension. The dogs kept their ruffs up in long spiny rows as they pranced back and forth and barked and growled at unseen dangers. A short distance away in the woods, an owl hooted or a turkey gobbled and was answered back. Occasionally a peeled head with its topknot and white-and-black-striped face appeared in an opening in the woods, or a warrior stalked from behind a tree.

The white man was getting a taste of the trying days of the Kentucky frontier. Manpower in many of the stations was small. At Hinkston's there were too few riflemen to stand off a heavy raid, and the settlers were forced to abandon their blockhouses and move back to McClelland's Station. Women and children with pack horses hastened on ahead under a light guard. A small band of men, led by Simon Kenton, covered their retreat. When the last settler was safely out of the way, Simon and his companions moved on to the stronger fort.

From this new post Simon again went to the woods as hunter and scout. The approaching fall and winter of that year found him hunting in a wide circle before all the stations. It was a comforting sight at McClelland's to see his drab figure disappearing into the woods. Behind him, he left assurance that the post would be fairly safe from a surprise raid.

Every man who knew the Kentucky woods realized in that year the time had come for the white man to decide whether he would defend his settlements or retreat beyond the mountains. The woods were full of warriors bent upon missions of terror against him. Already Governor Hamilton was using a successful and powerful force in Kentucky to pry wide open the back door of the American Revolution.

CHAPTER 13

With Boone And Clark In Kentucky

At Harrod's Station, George Rogers Clark lived up to his promise that he "would lend a helping hand if necessary." He spent his time learning about the new country. With the keen appraising eye of a surveyor, he was able to look forward to a day when Kentucky would be a thickly settled part of Virginia. His Virginia pride swelled up in him. He knew the time would come when the rich lands of the western country would be a bustling part of the great system of colonial states. It was too rich a prize to lose. Clark was quick to take up the argument with Henderson's grasping company. He looked upon Richard Henderson as a trespasser on Virginia soil, soil which had always been Virginia's. Efforts to organize an independent government at Boonesborough, however, threatened to destroy that colony's control. Young Clark was the best organizer west of the mountains. He formed a plan to destroy the dangerous Transylvania Colony and at the same time to end the threats to Kentucky from the outside.

Rivalry between Virginia and Richard Henderson's Transylvania was purely a political matter, which would be settled in due time. For Simon Kenton and his fellow frontiersmen, there were other matters of greater importance. Already

Simon knew that the pressure of the Indian attacks was growing with each succeeding raid. Soon the natives' bitter fight to save the caneland as a hunting ground would make futile every political issue. At the moment protecting Kentucky was a matter of keeping one step ahead of the war parties which crossed the Ohio. Time and again Simon covered the advance of a band of raiders, but he lacked the maturity and foresight to look into the future. As he rushed through the woods to carry vital warnings to settlers, he did not understand why the Indians continued their raids. He knew, of course, that they did not want to lose their hunting ground. What he did not understand was the power that was pushing them on. In this matter, the more experienced Clark had greater political understanding than his young friend.

While Simon was hunting for the Hinkston settlers and enjoying his last free moments in the great woods in the Licking valley, Clark was back in Virginia observing the troubled state of colonial affairs east of the mountains.

On every hand dissatisfaction with the English government was rapidly approaching the breaking point. All the young surveyor's friends were in the struggle. Thomas Jefferson had found the argument with the crown to his liking. Patrick Henry had openly defied the king's unhappy rule on two famous occasions, and every week he was gaining in political popularity in Virginia.

In hushed circles Virginians everywhere were whispering behind their hands of the revolution. At the same time that they spoke in opposition to the crown, they opposed Richard Henderson's colonial scheme in the western colony. Even Governor Dunmore, in the midst of his quarrell with his colonial subjects, had spoken bitterly of Henderson. Because of his love of a vast domain, the governor wished Kentucky to remain a part of Virginia.

All this information was invaluable to the Virginian. When Clark left home early in the spring of 1776 to recross the mountains, he knew pretty well what was to happen on the frontier. On the long stretches of woodland trail he had an opportunity to apply his mind to the problems of the western country. Men like Simon Kenton could not go on indefinitely defending settlers from Indian raids. Soon so many warriors would cross the Ohio, that even these gallant woodsmen were sure to be caught in a spreading net of war and butchery. There was need for organization on the part of the settlers to meet all the dangers facing them. He decided to call a meeting and ask each station to send delegates. They could organize a government and place their worries squarely before the Virginia Assembly.

Back in Kentucky, Clark learned of the hard winter. He heard of the retreat from Hinkston's and the siege of McClelland's. There were tales of horror and hardships on every hand. The time had come to act. A call for delegates to meet at Harrod's on June 6 was sent to the stations. When the assembly met, George Rogers Clark was absent. The delegates acted upon what they believed to be his wishes and appointed him and John Gabriel Jones to represent them before the Virginia Assembly. They were to go to Williamsburg to secure such assistance as they could.

That spring and summer had brought a stream of new settlers. While Simon Kenton was guiding them over the trails and serving as volunteer Indian scout along the Ohio River, Clark and Jones made their way to Williamsburg. Their journey was a difficult one, and they were delayed along the way. The Virginia Assembly adjourned. Already the colonies had declared themselves independent of the mother government, and the American Revolution was getting under way. This was a bad time to try to interest Virginia officials in the wild and sparsely settled Kentucky country. Governor Patrick Henry was ill and away from Williamsburg. George Rogers Clark was faced with a problem that required positive action. At the bedside of the sick governor he made a fervent plea for aid to Kentucky. Governor Henry was in sympathy with his request and sent Clark to the Council to secure a grant of powder and lead.

The Kentucky leader was fired with the belief that Virginia should make a powerful effort to protect the frontier. Before the Council he again presented a stirring argument, but his hearers were indifferent. Clark was disturbed. He never did things in the wishy-washy way of diplomatic Virginians. When the stubborn members made an impossible, selfish request of him, Clark's temper was aroused, and he uttered the blunt statement that a country not worth defending was not worth claiming.

The Council gave the two Kentucky delegates five hundred pounds of powder and lead to be delivered to them at Fort Pitt. At that point Clark and Jones were to take it aboard a canoe and deliver it in Kentucky at the "big landing" at Limestone.

They did not leave Virginia, however, until much later. News reached them that Judge Richard Henderson and his associates were working fast to get their settlement recognized as a fourteenth colony. Henderson was a shrewd politician, and there was danger that he might even win the Virginia Assembly to his point of view. Clark still had some arguing to do. He knew that Kentucky was now threatened both in Virginia and along the Ohio.

It was late fall before Clark and Jones felt it safe to leave for the West. At Fort Pitt there were many Indians. They lolled about in the trading posts, watched the river landings, and camped along every trail. Drowsy warriors sprawled before their camps or dozed along the water front. Clark and his companion knew they were spies, spies who had come to Fort Pitt to check

on the departure of settlers downriver for Limestone. News had already reached the braves that Clark and Jones were going to run the river gantlet with a cargo of powder and lead. All up and down the stream war parties were on the watch for the passage of the Kentuckians' canoe.

Along the riverbanks as they drifted downstream, Clark and Jones caught frequent glimpses of Indians. The branches of bushes growing at the water's edge parted for an instant and a painted face peered out at them. A branch quivered, and the bronzed heal of a warrior could be seen disappearing in the brush. Sometimes from upstream there came the faint sound of paddle strokes, or the tip of a canoe prow showed itself for a brief moment around a bend. The nearer to Kentucky they came, the tighter the net was being drawn. To land five hundred pounds of powder and lead and try to escape the vigilance of the Indian was folly. Clark had to devise a scheme for eluding their pursuers.

The precious cargo was divided into several parcels, and before the canoe reached Three Islands, Clark and Jones had planned their escape. As they passed the tip of the first island, their pursuers grew bolder. The war canoe came into full view. The Indians were crowding in for the capture. There was not the remotest chance to land openly on the Kentucky mainland and escape. The powder and lead had to be hidden on one of the Three Islands. Drifting to the lower end of the third island, the white men deposited the parcels of powder and lead on the bank and allowed their empty canoe to drift downstream.

Once ashore, Clark and Jones quickly hid their cargo in several different places and covered their tracks. When their pursuers followed the drifting canoe, the two white men crossed over to Kentucky and made their way hurriedly through the woods to McClelland's Station.

Simon Kenton was scouting the woods for signs of war parties and for meat with which to supply the settlements. He was present at the station when Clark arrived. When he heard the story of the powder and lead, he advised Clark not to try to bring it through the woods until a bigger force of men could be assembled.

There were too many Indians who knew about the shipment of powder to take any chance of losing it. The few guns at McClelland's were not enough to withstand a strong attack. Simon went as a guide with Clark to Harrod's Station to secure additional aid.

While they were gone, the headstrong John Gabriel Jones assumed leadership at McClelland's and organized a party to go with him to Three Islands to secure the powder. Jones knew too little of the woods to lead the party himself, and there was not a single good scout there. The party set off into the wilderness without sending a scout to cover the trail ahead of them.

Throughout the winter the Indians drifted into the Kentucky woods to attack the settlers. It was Christmas Day, and the barren woods were frozen. John Gabriel Jones and his men were many times exposed to open view of warriors, who darted undiscovered from one tree to another along their route. Near the Licking River the shrewd Mingo chief Pluggy intercepted the white party, and Jones and a companion were killed. Two men were taken prisoner, and the others rushed back badly defeated. They had exposed their station to an open attack. Pluggy and his braves were quick to follow up their advantage with a drive on the station itself.

When Clark and Simon Kenton arrived from Harrod's they found the station besieged. Simon was active in the fight. He used all his knowledge of Indian fighting to drive the Mingoes back into the woods. John McClelland was killed, and the whites killed Chief Pluggy. The Indian's death was a decisive blow, and his braves deserted the field of battle.

When the Indians left McClelland's Station, Simon and Bates Collier followed close on their heels to make certain that they would not turn back to make a surprise attack. At the Ohio the two scouts discovered that the Indians had crossed the river and knew that this time the Indians were out of the country. From the Indian crossing Simon and Collier made a flying trip to the Three Islands cache and found that the powder was safe. They made a record trip from McClelland's to the Ohio, to Three Islands, and back to Harrodsburg through the Indian-infested woods in five days. Clark immediatly organized a party to deliver the powder to the settlements.

Simon Kenton was chief scout on the journey to bring the powder across the Kentucky. His knowledge of the woods was a decisive factor in the return route chosen by the party. Simon used his knowledge of alternate trails to a good advantage. He always objected to taking an unnecessary risk, and when it came to a matter of matching wits with the Indians in the woods, he gave strict attention to every small detail. There at Three Islands he was more cautious than ever. Upon his shoulders largely rested the fate of the settlements. One small mistake and all would be lost.

Five hundred pounds of gunpowder and lead were precious everywhere in the colonies, but not nearly so much so as in the Kentucky woods. In the hands of crack backwoods riflemen under able leadership, this small supply of powder and lead could save Kentucky.

As his companions stood arguing over the best route to take going back, young Simon was making plans of his own. With grim determination he refused to let the party go directly to Harrod's. He knew the only way the powder could be delivered was to follow a long and circuitous trail. The journey before them was a mean one, but a few days later Simon proudly ushered his companions and their precious freight into Clark's cabin. It was a major step toward saving Kentucky from the Indians. Because of the safe delivery of the powder, the bloody year of the "three sevens" saw the Kentuckians withstand the frequent Indian attacks.

McClelland's Station was deserted. Some of the families went to Boonesborough, where they were joined by a party of frightened settlers, and later they returned east of the mountains. Long ago, settlers had moved into forts from their solitary cabins in the woods. The woods were alive with war parties. Governor Hamilton's influence was great, and the painted braves were running from one fort to the other, trying to catch the settlers off guard.

George Rogers Clark's jaw had a determined set. His eyes looked straight ahead, and a shadowy trace of deep concern was visible upon his face. Kenton clenched the tip of his musket barrel tightly with one hand, while he fingered the handle of his hunting knife with the other. Both he and Clark realized the time had come for the white man to make a determined stand or to fall back in permanent defeat. Simon knew the Indian blows would become heavier. He was finding it increasingly difficult to get through the woods. Every treetop, every trunk, and every bush was a possible hiding place for a skulking native. He had been forced many times of late to resort to night hunting in order to avoid walking into a trap.

Back in Virginia Clark's blunt arguments against Henderson had been heeded. Before he and Jones could land their cargo of gunpowder at Three Islands, Kentucky County had been created. Provision was made for an organized Kentucky militia, and George Rogers Clark was given the rank of major.

Since Kentucky was under the political direction of Virginia, its war was likewise that of the mother colony. Simon found himself in a new position in this remote political change. Clark became his commanding officer, and he in turn became an official scout entrusted with the duty of protecting the stations from surprise raids.

By the end of the winter the settlers were without food and clothing. Major Clark made plans to conserve everything the forts would need. Back at Hinkston's the settlers had grown a crop of hemp and flax. In the hot fall days before they had deserted the station, the plants were cut and spread upon the ground to rot. Before flax or hemp can be spun and woven, the fiber has to be broken away from the woody part of the plant. This was done during the sunny days of late February and early March.

Major Clark sent Simon with a small party of men to break out the flax and hemp and to deliver the fiber to Boone's and Harrod's stations. In the company was John Haggin, a reckless Dutchman always ready to take a chance. Near Hinkston's blockhouse he dashed ahead of the party to spy out the lay of the land. He was a hotheaded fellow, who at times was careless

and left his fellows openly exposed to Indian attacks. In his mad ride he discovered a large war party lying about the blockhouse. Simon advised his men to make immediate plans to retreat and to warn the stations of the approach of the Indians, because his force was too small to meet the Indians in an open fight in the woods. But Haggin was foolhardy to the last. He called Simon a coward for proposing to run away without giving the Indians at least one shot. Never before had anyone called the young woodsman a coward, and Simon's quick Irish temper flared. For a moment he forgot himself. Instead of retreating as he knew it was wise to do, he snapped back at Haggin that he was "ready to go as far and fire as freely as any man." A cautious young Dutchman in the party had remained astride his horse. He argued that the proposed attack would be suicide and said that he was ready to run.

The Indians had seen Haggin and rushed the white party.

Haggin was cowed and quickly took cover. Other members of the party fled at the first firing. Fortunately no one was killed.

Simon escaped into the woods. He knew the large war party meant that the Indians had crossed the Ohio to make a heavy drive against the forts. His companions rushed back toward Harrod's to carry a warning of the impending attack, but Simon went on to Boonesborough, making a dash through the woods that was perhaps his finest piece of woodsmanship. He traveled over a route closely watched every step of the way by warriors. So hot was the pursuit that when he arrived near the fort, he did not dare run across the clearing to the gate. For three or four hours he remained under thick cover awaiting an opportunity to warn the settlers of their danger. He became restless and sneaked up to the edge of the clearing to see what was happening. Across from him three or four settlers were bringing in the bodies of two men who had been caught alone on the trail. These men had been killed on the same trail over which Simon had traveled just a few hours before.

These were dark days for Kentucky. Had it not been for a few brave men like Kenton, Boone, Clark, James Ray, and Benjamin Logan, the forts would have surrendered, and the people would have gone back east. Every week the gloomy prophecy of Kentucky as "a dark and bloody ground" was coming true. It was now a common occurrence for parties to come running up to fort gates with wounded companions in their arms or dragging behind them the lifeless forms of companions whose scalps were missing. Despair had settled down upon Kentucky, and the end seemed surely to have come.

Then came starvation. Hunters hardly dared go into the woods. Even the most skillful scout found it almost impossible to escape being killed. When a hunter shot a deer or a buffalo, he was afraid he would be attacked before the carcass could be dressed. Transporting the meat to the fortress in any considerable quantity was out of the question.

During the spring and summer of 1777, the raiders lay in hiding about the forts and the settlers were able to grow little corn. At all three of the forts, it was the same story: the people were faced with starvation. Long periods of hunting in the wilderness had fitted Simon Kenton for just such an emergency. During these trying months he had many opportunities to prove himself superior even to the Indians as a woodsman.

Major Clark was quick to meet the military needs of Kentucky by appointing two scouts to serve each of the three forts. He chose Simon Kenton and Thomas Brooks to go to the major post at Boonesborough. Kenton and Brooks were given the responsibility of patrolling the woods between the Kentucky and the Ohio to prevent surprise approaches of war parties. Simon was back on his old stamping ground. He turned to the woods a very proud man. To be scout for the great woodsman Daniel Boone was evidence that he was highly trusted.

During the months which followed at Boonesborough, Simon thoroughly proved himself a game fighter. He and Brooks came in from the woods. It was April. Around the big fort the sycamores were putting out buds. Just beyond the south wall, the Kentucky was running flush after the early rains. Tall winter grass was stretching up its sharp green blades in a thick carpet, and on all sides the cardinal was dashing from tree to tree in blurred streaks of red, calling out in its plaintive notes that it was corn-planting time. Early one morning the cows had been milked and turned into the open field to graze. Instead of going to the field, they were nervous and stood around with their heads up and their ears forward. Their bulging eyes were staring anxiously into the woods. Squire Boone's "Old Spot," a good Indian detector, was unusually restless. She uttered low grumbling sounds, punctuated now and then with frightened snorts, and she lifted and dropped her tail as if awaiting the arrival of trouble to make her escape.

Inside the fort Boone and his companions were somewhat disturbed by these strange actions. But with customary frontier carelessness in the face of grave danger, they did nothing to prepare for an attack. Two men who had sauntered away from the stockade to get their horses stumbled on the Indians. They broke and ran for the gate, but the fleet-footed Shawnees overtook one of them and tomahawked him.

At the moment of the first firing, Simon Kenton and two other men were standing in the gateway with loaded guns. Simon rushed out and killed the Indian who had tomahawked the settler. When Daniel Boone heard the first shots, he came rushing out with a company of riflemen at his heels. Simon wheeled around to meet them and discovered an Indian drawing a deadly bead on Boone. Long ago he had learned to load his gun in an instant, and quickly he jerked his rifle to his shoulder and shot the second Indian. By this time a party of screaming warriors was closing in behind the whites to cut them off from the gate. Daniel Boone yelled for the whites to break for the fort and to sell their lives as dearly as possible. Simon reloaded his rifle, but while he was doing so, an Indian's bullet had broken Boone's ankle. Simon again shot a threatening brave. But before he could get to Daniel, a warrior rushed up with a drawn knife to slash the highly coveted scalp from the crippled woodsman's head. Simon "clubbed" his rifle and brained the Indian. Then he gathered the wounded man up in his arms and ran inside the gate to safety.

The women, led by Jemima Boone, carried Daniel to his cabin and bound his injured ankle with crude splints and leather thongs. When he was at last able to ease his pain, he sent for Simon. As Simon stood by the famous Long Hunter's bedside, Boone ran his broad hand up and down the youth's athletic arm. "Well, Simon," said he in his slow backwoods drawl, "you have behaved like a man today. Indeed you are a fine fellow." Simon had now risen to the proud estate of master scout knighted by Daniel Boone in good frontier style.

The fight before Boonesborough was fast and furious. Simon fought with great cunning and iron courage. By reloading his rifle the moment it was empty, his nimble fingers saved the day. Twice within a few moments he had saved Daniel Boone's life, and he had dropped four warriors in their tracks.

Two more bitter attacks were made by Shawnees on Boonesborough in the next few weeks, and Simon was on hand both times to help turn Chief Blackfish and his braves back into the woods. All this fighting brought heavy losses to the people at Boonesborough. Livestock and crops were lost. The Indians lingered about the forts until it was too late to do much planting, and once again the settlers were thrown upon the dwindling resources of the woods. Once more Simon's rifle became a mainstay of Kentucky.

CHAPTER 14

Winter

The long, dry autumn of the year of the "three sevens" faded quickly into a barren, cheerless winter. The dark cloud of hunger and starvation hung heavy over the frontier stations. All the way from Limestone to Cumberland Gap, it was the same disturbing story of raid, pillage, and murder. During the past summer few settlers had dared to run the risky gantlet to reach Kentucky. For every family that had come over the trails, one or two families deserted. Simon Kenton was constantly on the alert, scouting before Boonesborough, and when the worst of the raids were over, he retired to Benjamin Logan's badly weakened fort. He had been attracted to this station by the gallant defense put up by its settlers. All summer Logan and his people had fought against impossible odds. By winter they were desperate for the services of a good woodsman to help bring in supplies of food.

With a pitifully small band of courageous riflemen, Logan had written at his little fort one of the thrilling chapters in border defense. Simon enjoyed sitting for hours and listening to the settlers' stories of how Logan singlehandedly had saved his people from defeat. His fort was first attacked early one morning while the women were milking a short distance from the fort. A hundred braves were in hiding about the stockade, and when the whites came out to milk, they were thundered down upon in a bloody surprise attack. One of the men standing guard was killed, and two were seriously wounded. Women ran with their milk buckets, with warriors at their heels ready to scalp them. Only by sheer good luck was the milking party able to reach the fort gate without further injury. When the heavy puncheon gate swung open, there was pandemonium inside.

Logan's riflemen were outnumbered ten or twenty to one. There had been fifteen men before the raid began, but three of them were lost in the first firing, and it was up to the remaining twelve to hold the besieging party at bay. Behind the walls of the fort women stirred the cabin fires into hot, blazing coals and ran leaden bullets for the guns. They loaded the extra rifles, while the girls and older children ran with them in fast relays to the men at their posts.

The little band put up a brave fight. Their accurate marksmanship kept the Indians away from the walls, but the pressure was too great. Logan knew that without help from the outside his people would have to surrender. The situation was desperate, and only a reckless chance would bring help. Messengers would have to sneak out of the fort under meager cover and make their way through the tightly drawn siege line. Even if this move succeeded, there was the long stretch of treacherous wilderness trail which led southward to Cumberland Gap, and beyond the gap were many tiring miles of mountainous trail leading to the settlements of the Holston and Clinch rivers. It was a grave undertaking and the chances were against its success. But the settlers had to take this opportunity or suffer a worse fate at the burning stake in an Indian council house. Without hesitation, Benjamin Logan called for a volunteer to go with him. Eleven frightened men shook their heads. Finally John Martin, out of shame that none was willing to make the sacrifice, agreed to go. Outside the wall of the fort, however, Martin's nerve deserted him, and he scrambled back to cover, leaving Logan to go on alone. Once beyond the enemy's lines, Logan hastened along the winding trail which led southeastward to the older settlements. Within a short time he was back with the heartening news that aid was on its way.

This was one of the bravest stories of the wild Kentucky frontier, the sort of story that caused Simon to sit on the edge of his split-log bench in excited interest. Here a great woodsman had matched wits with Indians on the warpath and had won. Simon looked upon the tall, athletic Logan as a brave border hero whose part in the settlement of the frontier would someday have an important place in its story.

The men at Logan's, at Boone's, and at Harrod's were ready to meet the enemy so long as they could hold a blazing rifle. All of them had fought already with great skill and determination, but the growing storm beyond the Ohio made the odds against them too great. The real source of their trouble was too far removed from the Kentucky country to be stopped with well-aimed rifles or by a brilliant piece of woods strategy. Before the Kentuckians could win, they would have to strike hard against the enemy at the source of his power.

Fighting in Kentucky had been governed solely by the attacks on the fortress gates. There was no planning against these attacks except for the construction of stockade walls. When a war party of Indians came pouring down upon a fort, the settlers went into defensive action. They placed their faith in their marksmanship and their stout log walls. Always the great advantage of planned surprise was with the enemy. This scheme of things had to be reversed if Kentucky was to be saved.

Sitting at his table in the huge room in the big corner blockhouse at Harrod's, George Rogers Clark developed a plan for future attack. Like Logan's race for help, it was a fantastic scheme. It would require steady nerves, hot fighting, and a lot of good luck for it to succeed. But the very audacity of the proposal was reason enough for its success. Kentucky could not stand another summer like that of 1777. He proposed to carry the fight far beyond the Ohio. He would strike the enemy before his own vulnerable front door. When the Indian attacks were hottest, he called in four of the most trusted scouts. With these woodsmen sitting before him, the young major disclosed just enough of his plan to secure their cooperation. The one thing he wanted to know at the moment was the situation at Kaskaskia and Vincennes.

Clark proposed to send two scouts to the western British posts to secure detailed information. There were several things he especially wanted to know. How many soldiers and Indians were there? How large was the French population? How strong were the fortifications? What were the best routes of travel? He would tell these men no more. They would have to place their faith in his good judgment and carry out his instructions without knowing all he had in mind. They were asked to draw lots to see who should go. Before him were Simon Kenton, Si Harlan, Samuel Moore, and Ben Linn. All four would have volunteered their services in a moment. This was a scouting opportunity of a lifetime. Four brown hands drew lots. Samuel Moore and Ben Linn were lucky.

Sorrowfully, Simon watched his two friends pack their hunting sacks, fill their powder horns, swing their rifles over their shoulders, and go into the woods. It was the sort of mission he loved to perform.

George Rogers Clark left Kentucky in October, and Simon went to hunt for the settlers at Logan's Fort. He found the southeastern Kentucky woods exciting. The rugged hills were like those he had roamed over beyond the Big Sandy. For a time the trails were practically clear of Indians, and life was once again free in the wilderness. As winter settled down, however, the weather became extremely unpleasant. Simon found it more and more difficult to secure meat for Logan's people.

December was an exceedingly cold month. Heavy snowfalls blocked the trails. Game lost its flesh and was scarce. The tiny supply of corn at the fort dwindled away, and starvation became as frightening a menace as the Indian raids. Such poor meat as the hunters could bring in was unsavory because the salt supply was exhausted. At Boonesborough the settlers had reached the point where they could no longer eat the leathery meat without being nauseated.

During the first week of January, Daniel Boone organized a saltmaking party to go to the Lower Blue Licks, where streams of salt-bearing water bubbled up through the broken strata of the earth. The ground outside the fort was covered with snow. Going through the woods away from the fort, Boone's men left a wide, dark trail in their wake. It was a bad time for men to be out, but there was little fear of an Indian attack. At the Lower Blue Licks, the party went to work cutting wood and carrying water from the springs. This water was boiled in an iron kettle until it evaporated, leaving particles of salt clinging to the metal sides.

Daniel Boone went to the woods to hunt for meat, unconscious of the fact that a party of Blackfish's warriors had crossed the Ohio with the hope that they could catch the settlers off guard at the fort. Before they could reach Boonesborough, however, they came on the saltmaking camp. First they surrounded Daniel Boone and took him captive, and then they captured twenty-nine of his companions.

News of Boone's capture traveled fast. Simon Kenton was at Logan's when he heard about it and with John Haggin hastened to the rescue. They followed the big war party as far as its crossing place of the Ohio. But there were many Indians, and they were too alert for only a couple of men to attempt a rescue. They turned back with their discouraging news. The blow had been a deadening one at the hard-pressed fort. In midwinter it had lost most of its men and their brave leader.

Simon enlarged his circle of scouting and hunting to make up for the lack of men. During the remainder of the winter, he roamed the woods around both forts. He felt responsible for the welfare of Boone's settlement.

At last a late, cold spring came. The snow and frost disappeared, but the picture in Kentucky was darker than ever. George Rogers Clark was in Virginia on a mysterious mission. Daniel Boone and his men had been taken away to an unknown fate. Even Simon was becoming disturbed. As he roamed the solitary woods on hunts, he began to wonder what it was that Clark had up his sleeve. He reasoned that his friend had something in mind for Kentucky. Simon went over every detail of the strange conference he had attended at the blockhouse at Harrod's when Moore and Linn were sent away to the northwest.

As the wet spring weeks passed, time arrived for the renewal of the Indian attacks, and Clark was still absent. The manpower in Kentucky was badly reduced, and the spirits of the people confined in the filthy stockades were at a low ebb. Few immigrants were coming over the trails. As he made his cautious way through the woods looking for meat, Simon tried to solve the riddle of Kentucky's defense.

Through some mysterious source Simon finally got word of George Rogers Clark. Perhaps a settler brought him the first confused gossip of the major's activities. Clark was on his way to Redstone and Fort Pitt to recruit volunteers for a campaign in Kentucky. This was exciting news, and Simon went up the Ohio to see what he could learn. On this journey he crossed over his old hunting ground beyond the Big Sandy and made his way quickly to the point of his first departure for Kentucky.

His return to the head of the Ohio was a homecoming. There he saw his friend Simon Girty. In the last year or two, however, Girty had become embittered at the white frontiersmen. At the end of Dunmore's War, he had been refused the coveted appointment of captain and was now on his way to live again with the Indians and to fight for the British.

This visit reminded Simon Kenton of a forgotten act. When the scouts were preparing to lead Dunmore's army into the woods, the governor had required each of them to take an oath of loyalty. Now the American Revolution had begun, but Simon found himself still a British subject when he wanted so much to be an American. There was an officer of the Pennsylvania militia stationed at the fort, and perhaps, he thought, he could undo Governor Dunmore's oath and swear his new allegiance.

He wanted to have a clear conscience when he went back to Kentucky to help protect its frontier. The next morning Simon walked into the commandant's house and asked that he be allowed to pledge his loyalty to the states. Proudly he stood before the officer and held up his hand as he repeated the oath of allegiance to the American cause.

Simon waited a day or two longer for news of Clark, but the travelers who came to Fort Pitt from Virginia had heard nothing of him. Perhaps he had changed his plans and was not returning to Kentucky by way of the Ohio after all. Simon wanted to get back to the woods, so he turned southward down the river.

Back in Kentucky, Simon resumed his scouting for the forts, but he anxiously awaited the arrival of Clark. At last the mysterious army appeared around the great bend of the Ohio and headed for the Limestone landing. Clark saw the drab figure of a lone buckskin hunter leaning on his rifle—it was Simon waiting at his station of two years before to greet his old friend. He was curious to know of Clark's plans for saving the Kentucky settlements. Why had he gone back to Virginia? What was his object in bringing men and their families from Redstone and Fort Pitt?

But Clark's plans for the future defense of the frontier were so hazardous that he could hope to succeed only by the utmost secrecy. He could not divulge its real objective even to so trustworthy a woodsman as Simon Kenton. Clark knew that even the most reliable frontiersmen were gossipy; if his plans were made known to one man, then there was danger of everyone, including the enemy, knowing them.

When his heavily loaded canoes had halted for a moment, Clark asked Simon to secure the volunteers in Kentucky to meet him either at the mouth of the Kentucky or at the Falls of the Ohio.

CHAPTER 15

Kaskaskia

At the forts Simon found the people hostile to the idea of sending volunteers to join Clark's army. Only Simon's hotheaded Dutch friend John Haggin agreed to go. A party of saltmakers under the leadership of the wordy Irishman Joseph Montgomery had established a salt camp at Drennon's Lick. Kenton and Haggin went to get them to go with Clark. When Montgomery heard their request, he and his ten men shouldered guns and went with the woodsmen to the camp on Corn Island. Kenton and Haggin were the only Kentuckians to volunteer their services for the Kaskaskia expedition.

At the rendezvous Clark was busy with plans for the drive against the British posts beyond the Ohio. He divided the men into four companies. Canoes were made ready, and when the fair weather of mid-June arrived, preparations for the departure were completed. Clark had Simon Kenton and John Haggin as dependable scouts. They were not assigned to the militia companies but were sent ahead to scout the lower Ohio River. On June 24 the sun was shining brightly. Below Corn Island the rising current of the river roared through the broken, rocky shoals of the falls. Clark's men pulled upstream a short distance so as to head their canoes into a running straight shot at the rapids. Before them, Kenton and Haggin wavered in and out of view as they covered the company's entrance into the treacherous shoals.

At the moment the lead canoe pitched into the rapids on a rising tide of water, the sun went into an eclipse. Looking back through the spray, Simon saw Clark's men rushing down behind him in the subdued light. When they rose and fell with the wash of the river, they appeared as heroic statues displayed on a vast, crude panorama. Clark, dressed in coarse buckskin with the brim of his broad beaver hat turned up in front, sat in the stern of one of the tossing canoes, a sturdy bronzed symbol of frontier determination.

Below the mouth of the Tennessee, at Fort Massac the canoes were abandoned. There Clark chose to go overland to the mouth of the Kaskaskia River. Here he secured additional information and the services of a trader who would guide his party to the British fort. Simon Kenton and John Haggin went with the guide, John Saunders, partly as assistants but largely as observers to guard against being led into a trap. Simon was present when the luckless Saunders became confused and momentarily lost his bearings. He heard George Rogers Clark, in a burst of ill-temper, upbraid the baffled guide and threaten him with severe punishment if within an hour he had not found the trail.

Saunders and his assistant guides proved efficient. Clark's little army was soon before the fort. They had made the long journey from the Ohio River without being detected. At a farmhouse across the river from the fort, they found a friendly settler from Pennsylvania, who gave them much useful information.

The wily Virginia leader was cautious. He planned immediately to make up in clever strategy for the force he lacked in men. His small number had to make every stroke count.

Under cover of darkness they would cross the Kaskaskia River, and when the fiddles were ringing loudest at the Creole dance, they would fall upon their enemy. Men were stationed all along the wall, and at a given signal they were to work their way through the village. A party of hand picked men was ordered to follow Clark to the commandant's house. When the backwoodsmen entered the house, they found Rocheblave and his wife asleep. So quietly did they make their entry into his bedroom, that the Canadian officer was unconscious that he was surrounded by the horrible Long Knives, whom he had so often described to his Creole neighbors. Simon Kenton stepped forward and took the slumbering commandant by the shoulder and roused him from his sleep to inform him that he was a prisoner of war. Without the firing of a single gun or the unsheathing of a single knife, Clark captured his first objective.

That night, while Frenchmen shuddered in their cabins and awaited the horrible fate they believed in store for them, Clark quickly planned his next move. Two hundred and forty miles to the east was Fort Vincennes. He needed information regarding the situation of this village, so he sent Simon Kenton and two of his companions to spy upon the British and Indian forces.

At Vincennes Simon and his weather-beaten companions concealed their hats and guns. For three nights, their blankets thrown over their shoulders Indian-fashion, they prowled through village streets. During this visit they had an opportunity to examine the fortifications in detail. When their scouting was finished, Bond and Batty hastened back to Kaskaskia to report their findings to Clark. Simon went on to Kentucky to inform Colonel John Bowman at Harrod's Fort of the success at the British post.

Clark entrusted an important secret message to Simon, knowing he was the one scout who could safely make his way

through the wilderness. He wrote his report to Colonel Bowman and packed it in Simon's hunting pouch. He took Simon aside and repeated the message orally to him. If Simon was threatened with capture, he was to destroy the written message.

Simon hastened to Harrod's Station from Vincennes, and then he went on to Boonesborough. When he arrived there, he found a demoralizing lull in the preparations for a siege. The men had grown restless. During the first few weeks after Daniel Boone and Hancock escaped their Indian captors at Chillicothe and came home to prepare the fort for an attack, there was great activity, but now a casual indifference had fallen over the place. Dirt from a half-dug well was piled high in the courtyard. An idle pick and spade lay at the bottom of the dry hole. Frontiersmen had decided that the attacks perhaps would not come, and they did not wish to perform any more work in the lazy summer weather than was necessary. Overhead the hot midsummer sun seemed to remain in one place and to send down its blistering rays.

Beyond the walls of Fort Boonesborough, the ground was baked to a grayish crisp. The luxuriant bluegrass had given up months before, and its brown mat was falling into dry decay. The Kentucky River was at a low stage, and every week more of the wide sand and pebble beach crawled up out of the water as the shrinking stream was crowded against the steep south bank. Leaves of the trees in the woods wilted and dropped in the midday heat. It was a time when ordinarily the settlers would have spent most of the hot hours sitting drowsily in the shade of the massive sycamores.

Inside the fort there was nerve-racking suspense. First, Daniel Boone's arrival had created panic. Men, women, and children went to work quickly to prepare for an attack. A party of men began work to complete the well. Lusty strokes of their heavy pick bit deep into the hardened dry loam of the river bottomland. Spades moved up and down, lifting the loosened dirt from the ever-deepening hole. In the wilting corn patches, men stripped tender green roasting ears from the stalks. Women and children drove in from the pasture as many of the cows as could be penned in the courtyard. A continuous string of buckets passed to and from the river. Water was being stored in every available vessel.

Daniel Boone was busy inspecting the walls of the fort. Green-log replacements were substituted for the older puncheons which were weakened by rot. Men carefully swabbed their guns. Tiny platform rifle stations were built at strategic points along the fortress walls for the men to stand on to fire at the enemy. Boone dictated a hurried note to the militia officers of the older settlements east of the mountains asking for help. On every hand was excitement. At any moment he expected Blackfish and his warriors to appear.

Days went by and the feverish pace of preparation began

to lag. Both Daniel Boone and William Hancock were positive that the Indians were coming. Out in front in the territory between Boonesborough and the Ohio River were no signs of a large war party of Indians. The pioneers became nervous, and some of them were short-tempered and quarrelsome. When Boone was captured at the salt licks in the winter, he had made extravagant promises to help the Indians later in the year if they would not attack Boonesborough at that time. Some of the settlers knew about this and suspected Daniel of treachery. They became more suspicious when he proposed to go over the Ohio to see what was happening.

Daniel Boone was worried. Neither he nor Simon could make a satisfactory guess as to what had happened to Blackfish and his army. There was only one way to find out. Daniel had learned much of the Indian system of espionage while a prisoner at Chillicothe. They kept a close check on the settlements in Kentucky. He now proposed to use the same system. He and Simon Kenton with a party of nineteen riflemen would spy on the Indians. Simon went ahead as war scout. The trail to Paint Creek led northward across the Ohio through the thickly wooded section of caneland beyond the river. Many times Simon found it difficult to make his way through the matted canes. Occasionally he had to turn his back to the trail and shove through by main force. Behind him, Boone's men took turns breaking trail. All about them were many Indian signs, but none indicated a large war party.

As signs of the Indians grew more numerous, Simon became more cautious, keeping himself well under cover so that he would not be exposed to a deadly surprise attack. He was careful to avoid falling into a trap. Simon knew that ahead of him was gathering a storm of war. Shrewd British and Indian leaders were plotting the destruction of the white Kentucky settlers, and they had spies throughout the woods. Eyes peered over logs, from behind trees, or from beneath clumps of bushes, and messengers went silently to the war councils with news of what they had seen. Around Simon the silence of the dark woods was oppressive. Occasionally it was broken momentarily by a bird which flitted past him with a nervous whirring of wings, or a fluted call came from high in the timber. Overhead the wide-spreading branches of the magnificent hardwood trees were interlocked. Here and there long shafts of warm sunlight poured through a leafy hole to splatter in a shimmering patch upon the ground.

For a brief moment Simon forgot the purpose of his mission as the silence of the great woods suddenly was broken. A tiny bell tied around an Indian pony's neck tinkled rapidly ahead of him, and then there was a thunderous burst of laughter. Immediately Simon recognized the harsh, guttural tones. Before him the bushes waved violently, and a galloping pony pitched into the open. Two young braves were astride the animal. One faced its tail and the other its head. This was an astounding spectacle. Never before had Simon seen such a sight. The young Indians were spurring the pony on, and it was kicking up its heels in bitter protest. The mischievous Indians were lost in the infectious spell cast by the thick forest land. They were headed straight for the spot where Simon was hiding. The two, sitting back to back, were moving into short rifle range. Was this a wild dream of the silent woods or was it a galloping reality? Simon's tense hands moved up and down the long, burly wooden brace of his gun. Perspiration dripped from his forehead. His teeth were clamped tightly over a rigid, dry tongue. Deliberately the heavy, thick-barrel rifle was eased upward as silently as the dancing sunspots in his path. Two Indians! Two scalps! Simon's temples were being pounded by a roaring surge of blood. His wildest dreams of Indian fighting had never brought them galloping to him in pairs lined up back to back. Slowly the gun was leveled into position. The long, hairlike foresight crept down to dead center of the V of the hindsight. Simon's strong right thumb pulled the long flintlock hammer back until a gentle, silent movement of the spring release told him the safty catch had moved into place. His nervous forefinger tightened on the trigger as his half-closed right eye kept the two sights centered on the approaching warriors. In a split second the silence of the deep woods was broken by the deafening roar of his rifle. The frightened pony reared on its hind legs and turned sharply around in its tracks. At its feet two braves were rolling and gasping frantically in their death throes. Simon's bullet had sent them toppling to the ground. One was dead and the other mortally wounded.

For a moment Simon forgot to be cautious. Impulsively he hauled out his scalping knife and rushed forward to claim the tokens of a border fight. Before he could reach the first Indian, there was a rustling in the cane. Simon saw a warrior taking aim, and within the nick of time he jumped aside. He took cover behind a tree, and before he could reload his gun, a dozen warriors surrounded the fallen Indians. The wounded man was taken away, and just as Simon was about to be shot by the infuriated warriors, Boone and his men arrived and drove them back into the cane. When the last Indian leaped for cover, Simon pressed forward and scalped the dead brave who had been left behind.

The two Indians riding toward Simon on the bucking pony had been members of a party going to join Blackfish at Chillicothe. Boone was certain of this, but he wished to make one more check. He sent Simon and Alexander Montgomery forward to spy on the Indian village at Paint Creek. Soon they returned with the information that there were no braves present. Only old men, women, and children moved about the cabins. Boone felt sure that the Indians were already on their way to raid

Boonesborough. He and his men rushed home to defend their settlement.

Simon and Montgomery remained in the woods to prey upon the deserted village. A single scalp was not enough of a trophy to take back to Kentucky. Simon was out to play the Indian's fast game of stealing horses. He and his companion raided the horse pound, and came away with four ponies. They rushed southward to Harrod's Fort with their prizes. This was a new type of adventure, and there were far too many Kentucky horses in the Indian corrals for them to forget.

There they learned that Boonesborough was already under seige and the two scouts went immendiately to its aid; when they arrived, the four hundred braves of Blackfish and de Quindre were milling about the stockade. No one could get through the line they had drawn about the fort, and there was great danger that Boone's sharpshooting riflemen would mistake Kenton and Montgomery for Indians. During the whole siege, the two scouts were behind the Indian line watching the fight. When at last rain came pouring down in great flying sheets, and the Boonesborough settlers dug a counter trench to prevent the fort from being undermined, the Indians gave up the fight. The big gate was pushed wide open, and Simon Kenton and Alexander Montgomery rushed in to greet the exhausted but victorious settlers. By the beginning of the seventh day, Blackfish and his dejected army were well on their way toward the Ohio.

CHAPTER 16

Mazeppa Ride

In late September 1778, three Kentucky scouts
Simon Kenton, Alexander Montgomery, and
George (not George Rogers) Clark—crossed the Ohio. They
traveled rapidly, and within a remarkably short time, they were
lying in wait before the Indian village of Chillicothe. There they
watched the Indians going about their affairs. Simon had visited
this village once before and knew its arrangement. Now the
scene had changed, for the warriors were at home. Simon made
a mental note of all he saw.

At Harrod's Fort Colonel John Bowman was making plans.
When Kentucky County was created, he had been appointed
county lieutenant, but his lack of courage and ability had made
him unpopular. Grumbling settlers accused him of lacking
common sense. Colonel Bowman was a proud man. His greatest
dread was that of being disgraced before the people of Kentucky.
He was determined to make a bold stroke. Clark had succeeded
by such a move at Kaskaskia, and he would do the same thing
in the Indian country. Clark went to Kaskaskia with complete
information on the fort, and before Colonel Bowman launched
a campaign outside Kentucky, he, too, needed much information.
Since he lacked the good judgment of the woods which had

distinguished the other leaders, he had to depend upon others.

The village of Chillicothe presented a perfect picture of peace and well-being. Drowsy warriors lolled around their crude cabins and tents. Children ran errands and performed simple chores. The women were busy with their many hard tasks. Even the army of village dogs had fallen under the drowsy influence of the sunny fall day, and they napped at their masters' feet. Just beyond where he was hiding, Simon located the corral. There were many fine horses; some of them had been stolen in Kentucky. It was a simple matter for the crafty woodsmen to sneak through the bars with a handful of salt and catch as many horses as they wanted. So long as there was salt, the animals would submit to having halters slipped over their heads without creating a commotion. But to break down the bars and rush away with the stubborn beasts was another matter. Simon had already worked out the strategy. When they had haltered the horses, they would make a bold break for the woods before the surprised Indians could get ready to follow them.

Inside the corral the Kentuckians became greedy. Each man picked out a horse to ride and haltered an extra one. Someone, however, caught three. There was a noisy rustle among the horses when they were ready to start. A loud warning shout went up that Long Knives were stealing horses. In an instant every Indian in the village was yelling at the top of his voice, and before the last bar of the pen had fallen to the ground they were in hot pursuit.

Ahead of the howling mob two excited white riders bent low over their mounts and tugged stoutly at their halter reins. The third white man rode madly in the rear whipping the snorting, stubborn horses into a wild gallop. They rode forward, crashing through the low undergrowth of the woods near the village. They were headed for thick cover. Behind them the din of the Indians grew louder. The race settled down to one of grim determination to see who could endure the chase longest and maneuver the fastest.

Simon and his companions were mounted bareback, and the flimsy halter reins were the only control they had over the galloping horses. Their long rifles, slung over their shoulders at the ends of long leather straps, swung back and forth in heavy tugging motions. Heartless branches of trees and bushes raked and scratched at their legs and faces. Now and then the heaving belly of a horse scrubbed a knee and thigh of a rider against the rough bark of a tree. The going was fast and rough, but only one thing mattered to the hotblooded Simon and the other two scouts. They had to outride the Indians at all cost and to save every horse they had captured.

As the mad rush kept up, the noise of the pursuers died away. The chase was too fast for the Indians on foot. The Kentuckians were in the clear and riding like mad. They pitched over a hill and moved down into the edge of a heavily wooded swamp.

Once behind the sheltering wall of thick timber, Simon and his companions had a moment in which to halt and catch their breaths. Their next move was to get across the Ohio as quickly as they could. No Indian would submit to the indignity of having his horses stolen. A party of warriors would be sure to get on their trail in an effort to head them off at the river.

From the swamp the three scouts moved cautiously toward Eagle Creek crossing. Overhead what had been a clear sky was now heavily overcast. The Ohio country was about to have its first cold, blowing rain of fall. Autumn wind- and rainstorms blew up quickly along the river. When there was a gale of wind, big waves rolled in a heavy tide against the riverbanks. Then only an experienced woodsman could hope to cross the stream safely.

When Simon's party reached the crossing, the wind was

blowing hard. Pounding waves were being swept high against the north bank. Every wild gust of the autumn wind slapped huge sheets of water in their faces. Their rearing horses refused to attempt the crossing.

Ever since the day Simon first reached the western woods, with one exception, he had exercised great caution in everything he did. But the wild ride from Chillicothe had intoxicated him. It was not the clever Simon of Three Islands who had arrived at Eagle Creek. Here he committed the first of a series of costly blunders. Instead of giving up the idea of crossing the river and riding downstream until the storm let up, he and his companions hobbled their horses and spent the night near the river. After staking out the animals, the men doubled back on their trail for a safe distance to watch for the Indians.

Early the next morning they were back at the river. A raft was built to transport the guns across, and Simon prepared to swim along with the horses. The wind was still blowing and the waves were high, but after much whipping and yelling the horses were in the water. Simon swam along below them. A short way out in the stream, however, the animals turned back and Simon was forced to follow.

Back at the starting place, the three woodsmen realized that crossing the river was out of the question. They would select a good horse apiece and head for the Falls of the Ohio. If only Simon and his companions had followed this decision, they would have covered up their blunder of the day before. But when the extra horses were freed to return to the woods, the white men wished at once to recover them. Soon the party turned back to reclaim their mounts. This hesitation and loss of time violated the code of the frontier trail. It took time to round up stray horses. Before Simon and his companions could complete the recapture, there was a wild whoop. The Indians had arrived! Simon was unafraid, and for a moment he made the mistake of losing respect for the cunning of the natives. He dismounted, hitched his horse, and went back on foot. Before he reached the steep riverbank, three warriors and a white man rode toward him. They had not seen him, and using the tactics which had succeeded when he shot two Indians at once from the bucking pony, Simon aimed at the foremost rider. The long hammer of his gun came back with a dull click. An Indian rode squarely between his sights. Simon's long forefinger squeezed the trigger, and the clumsy flint scraped down beside the lock with a loud snap. Sparks from the flint sputtered brightly for an instant and then died away. Simon's faithful gun had flashed the pan. He had neglected to examine the priming after failing to cross the river. His gun had been drenched aboard the raft, and now it failed him.

The alert Indians heard the telltale clicking of the gun. In the next moment they were charging forward to capture Simon. He dashed into the thick woods and took cover behind some fallen timber. Once again he hoped to evade his pursuers in a wild run, but this time it was they who were mounted. Simon was quickly surrounded. When he broke from cover a mounted brave rushed up to him holding out his hand and shouting "Brother! Brother!" Simon's gun was clogged with wet powder, and here was an Indian calling him brother. He "clubbed" his rifle and prepared to strike the warrior a deadly blow. Before he could do this, two strong hands caught his shoulders, and a bony knee was thrust into his back. Simon was a prisoner. He had fallen a victim to his own foolhardiness. Recent successes had gone to his head, and he had come to believe that he could forever escape the Indians.

While the warriors were struggling with Simon, Alexander Montgomery rushed up and fired at them. His shot went wild, and it served only to expose him to their wrath. As Simon was being bound, several of the Indians went to capture Montgomery.

There was a loud shot; a moment later there was a second. Simon knew what had happened. One shot had missed. The second had reached a deadly mark. A little later the warriors came back with a blood-matted scalp and slapped it in Simon's face and threatened him with a similar fate. He knew that a short distance away the mangled body of his friend lay exposed to the weather and the ravages of animals. For him, a living prisoner, there was to be an even worse fate. Clumsy, short-waisted George Clark, the poorest woodsman of the three, made his escape.

Kenton was well known around the council fires as an able scout. On many occasions he had brought defeat to parties because he had reached the settlements in time to warn of the raid. Worst of all, Simon had been caught stealing horses in broad daylight from right under the noses of the braves. Shawnee tempers were quick and their patience was short. They lambasted him for being a horse thief. In a mad rumbling tirade of broken English, a warrior abused him because he was a white man. "You steal horse! Hey!" they shouted in angry outburst. They snatched him around by his hair, whipped him with their drawn ramrods, and threatened him with death by tomahawking.

The Shawnees knew that Simon was a clever man. They could not afford to take chances with him. In one brief moment of carelessness he might get the drop on them and run away, because on several occasions he had proved that with an even break he could outrun the Indians. It was late in the afternoon and the braves resolved to play safe. They would spend the night on the bank of the Ohio. Simon was forced to stretch himself flat on his back upon the ground. This was the torture known to frontiersmen as being "stretched out." His arms were pulled out to full length and a heavy stick was laid across his chest. Buffalo thongs were strapped tightly around his wrists and looped securely to the stick. Two stakes were driven down at his feet, his legs were pulled apart and heavy tugs fastened tightly over his ankles and strapped to the stakes. A noose was placed around his neck and drawn up snugly under his chin and then fastened to a bush. While he was being tied, the Indians kept up their bitter scolding. They slapped and whipped him. In every breath they cried out at him for stealing their horses.

The storm chilled the Ohio woods at night. Simon was cold. His arms felt as though they would drop from his shoulders. His legs ached all the way to his hips. Wherever the leather thongs bound him, they bit into his skin and made ugly red imprints where the circulation was checked. The tingling, sleepy feeling in his feet and hands was maddening. Simon's back rested heavily upon the uneven ground. Roots and twigs bit their cruel way into his skin. When the wind died down, mosquitoes and gnats swarmed over his throbbing body. Every impulse prompted him to draw up his legs and arms, but the slightest movement sent agonizing pains coursing through his body. Long after the braves had ceased their wild dancing around Montgomery's scalp, Simon could hear their peaceful snoring. This long night of cruel suffering was only a beginning. In the morning he would be subjected to new and inhuman tortures.

A wild, unbroken horse was led into camp in the morning. Its shaggy mane and tail, heavy with burrs, showed that it had never been ridden. Simon was about to be given a Mazeppa ride. This form of torture had originated in Poland, when Ivan Stephanovich was strapped back down on a wild pony. Amidst a great babble of laughter and abuse, the Indians cut Kenton's leather bindings and jerked him from the ground. Two or three braves held the rearing horse while the others pushed him astride it. His aching feet and legs, which felt heavy and swollen when he was placed in an upright position, were caught in the loop of a heavy leather band and bound securely under the belly of the animal. Simon's arms were drawn behind him and securely bound. A running bowline was passed around the neck of the horse, looped around Simon's and tied under the horse's tail as a crupper. To top off the prisoner's mountings, a pair of moccasins were hung over his hands so that he could not push aside limbs and briars. For his tormentors Simon's unhappy predicament was real sport. In a few moments he would run the risk of losing his life without even a sporting chance of fighting back.

When the unbroken horse was turned loose, it bucked and charged forward and backward, trying to shake the reeling prisoner from its back. It reared on its hindlegs and came down in frantic side bucks and mad whirls. Simon's helpless body, held in place by the leather bindings, reeled back and forth. Briars and thornbushes tore his clothes and gouged mercilessly at his flesh. Low-hanging branches scratched his face and dealt him stunning blows. Every jump of the horse lifted him up and dropped him down upon its rigid back with disjointing shocks. Simon's legs were so trussed that he could not use his knees to brace himself against the nervous lunges of the horse. As the body expanded and retracted under the heavy breathing of the winded animal, the thongs bit deeper into the raw bands around the rider's legs. Simon wove back and forth with every movement. He reached the point of waiting and hoping to die. Courageous as he was, this torture was too much for even a strong man to bear. Mercifully, the pony soon settled down to a steady jog in line with the other horses of the party. All day Simon reeled back and forth astride his mount. His suffering was even greater than it had been during the night before.

When the Indians made camp on the second and third nights, they again stretched him out, and for hours they kept up a war dance around him and around the hoop on which Montgomery's scalp was stretched. Simon stared at the scalp and envied Montgomery. During the daytime rides this gruesome token of Indian warfare was always there to mock him. Simon's body had already taken enough punishment to kill an ordinary man. But he was stouthearted, and he still had a faint hope that his captors would misjudge his strength and he could break away to freedom.

On the second day he was trussed to his horse, but the animal was gentler and did much less bucking than on the day before. Simon realized that the party was covering ground quickly. He knew that at nightfall they were within sight of the village at Chillicothe. The braves, however, were not going on. They were going to wait until morning to make a proud entry. They were taking home a rich prize that would make their return a triumphant one.

When the sun came up, there would be the delights of the long gantlet in which brutal clubs, switches, and knives would swing with insane vengeance. The Indians would shout with delight as they pounded their prisoner with heavy blows. Council fires would blaze up, and about them imposing chiefs would make long and impasssioned speeches begging for the most savage torture of the white Kentuckian.

Drooped over in his cramped, painful position, Simon knew as well as did the Indians what was in store for him at the end of his journey. He was advancing toward his first running of the gantlet. He knew that soon there would be a shrill scalp yell announcing their arrival, and the deafening beats of leather clubs upon the tom-toms in the village would answer. There would be wild cheering by a band of men, women, and children, which would be heard above the noise of the drums. For Simon the bedlam of noise would be a terrifying signal of death.

CHAPTER 17

Running The Gantlet

When Simon's captors came within a mile of Chillicothe, they halted to make camp for the night. But, impatient, the warriors could not wait for morning to receive the praise of their people. Runners went ahead to make known the fact that the party had returned with the stolen horses, a scalp, and a prisoner. All the inhabitants came running to the night camp. Men, women, and children surrounded the bound prisoner. Soon a wild dance was going, and Simon suffered abuse by being kicked and whipped.

Chief Blackfish came to question the prisoner. He was smarting from his failure to take Boonesborough. Daniel Boone's escape from Chillicothe and his trickery in Kentucky were humiliating. Blackfish was furious at the way his friend Boone had treated him, and he wanted to know if Simon acted under Boone's orders. When Simon assured him that he was not associated with Boone and had stolen the horses of his own free will, the chief gave him a severe whipping. Every stroke of the rough switch left long, ugly red marks. Here and there splotches of blood oozed from the wounds. Blackfish was making up on Simon's back some of the losses which had come to him because of his raid against Kentucky.

The whipping was the beginning of long hours of extreme punishment. Simon was tied to a stake, and the women snatched his clothing. A wild shouting mob danced around him, kicking and switching his bleeding body. In another circle warriors again jumped and skipped around the hoop containing Alexander Montgomery's scalp. When at last the dance had ended and Simon was on the verge of sinking into a state of unconsciousness, he was untied from the stake and again stretched out. The Indians went back to the village, and Kenton was left to suffer torment from the swarms of gnats and mosquitoes which sucked at his wounds.

In the morning Simon was released from the ground by the excited braves who were anxious to be on their way toward the village. The loud scalp yell was sent up, and Simon was ordered to begin walking to a new series of tortures.

From down the trail came a rising babble of angry sounds. All during the night, visitors had poured into the village to be present for the sport. Tribal anger was whipped to a new high pitch. Everyone was angry and shouting bitter Shawnee oaths at the white man. On every hand were waving switches and clubs with which to beat the prisoner. When Simon approached the village, he saw a long weaving line of two columns stemming out from the door of the council house.

Before him was the long gantlet of attackers waiting to whip him to death. Yet Simon knew that other frontiersmen had lived through these lines of terror. He was still strong, even if the last three days had sapped much of his strength. His muscles were drawn and irritated. The places where the leather thongs bound him were too sore to touch. Simon was going into his first gantlet with a handicap. If he were fresh he could escape, but his muscles were cramped and stiff, and he could not dodge and run fast enough to avoid being beaten.

He remembered some advice a friendly Negro named Caesar

had once given him. Caesar had often watched prisoners make the run and had come to appreciate the fine points of defending oneself. To run straight down the middle of the gantlet was to invite death. There was a trick. If the prisoner crowded in close to one of the lines and stayed as far from the other as possible, he could cause a lot of confusion among the Indians and avoid most of the heavy blows. Standing before the gantlet, Simon ran over in his mind all the advice which Caesar had given him. He knew the Indians were sporting. If a prisoner could break through the ranks and get to the council house without being stopped or hit, he would not have to run the gantlet over.

When Simon's captors pushed him forward to the head of the gantlet, he began a survey of the situation before him. There were two lines of the angriest human beings he had ever seen. Even the children were storming about him. Far down the line an enraged brave waved a keen knife. If Simon passed that point, he would be maimed and beaten to death. Somewhere before he reached the brave he must break through and escape. He would hurl his heavy body against an unsuspecting woman or child and rush for the council house.

At the foot of the gantlet a drummer kept up a monotonous clatter of torture and death. The moment for starting came. Simon looked down the line and became weak in the face of it. Heavy drops of perspiration ran from his face. It seemed too much to ask a human being to hurl himself into that storm of cruelty. Behind him two braves with sharp knives made certain he would not turn back. Suddenly a hush fell over the crowd. Arms were upraised. Long flails were poised. Simon leaned forward ready to make his plunge. In a second the loud drum tap sounded, and he was away to run his first gantlet.

Simon ran fast. Blows fell on him from all sides. His strategy of crowding up close to one line kept most of them from hitting him squarely. Just before he reached the point where he had seen

the knife, he plunged through the line and headed for the council house in a wild dash. He was not to go entirely free, however, for two braves landed blows. Near the door he was met by a warrior draped in a blanket who chased him and threw him to the ground. The infuriated mob rushed up and beat him almost to death. His clothes were again jerked off, and when the storm of blows had subsided, Simon lay upon the ground exhausted and unconscious. He was so nearly dead that he could not return to the gantlet without being killed.

But there were to be other celebrations, and the councils of braves were not ready for Simon to die. They revived him and gave him food and drink so that he would recover sufficient strength to run other gantlets.

Almost from the moment of Simon's capture on the Ohio, it was a foregone conclusion that he should be burned at the stake. No decision had been made, however, as to time and place.

He was no ordinary Kentucky cabin settler, and to destroy him at once would deny all the other villages the privilege of punishing him. Simon was to be used to stir up the wrath of the tribes against the white man. The exhibition of the famous white scout in the villages might redeem some of the prestige lost by the war parties in their luckless raids on Kentucky. The torturing of a prisoner in the long gantlet gave great satisfaction. Eventually there would come the grand climax when he would be destroyed at the stake amid the loud screams and yells of the tribes.

Simon was taken into the council house. Seated before him was a large circle of grunting warriors. Their peeled heads and stiff topknots bobbed up and down as they turned to scowl at him. In the center of the ring the flame of the council fire leaped toward the roof. A stolid chief sat in the place of honor near the center of the circle. At his feet were the symbols of the Indians' strength—a scalping knife and a war club. There were many speeches. Some of the orators were for delaying Simon's destruction until he had been paraded around the other villages. Others asked for the white man's life at once. When the speeches were ended, the chief handed the club to the circle of warriors. The club passed from one hand to another. Those who wished to burn Simon at the stake slammed it bitterly against the ground; those who favored waiting simply passed it on. A teller with a flat stick and the chief's knife followed the club around to record the vote by notches.

Kenton watched the procedure with interest. If he was to be burned at once, he had no hope of escape. If his execution was to be delayed by a journey around to the villages, there might be a chance to make a break and outrun his captors. Present with the Indians was a white man who had helped make him captive. Simon asked him what his fate was to be, and the man replied that he was to be burned at the stake.

The Indians now adopted a friendlier attitude toward the

prisoner. He was given good clothing and left unbound for the journey. They started for the central village of Wapotomika, where he was to be destroyed.

Between Chillicothe and the big council town of Wapotomika were two important villages, Pickaway and Machecheek. At each of these places Simon felt sure he would be forced to run the gantlet.

At Pickaway the Indians were lined up with their flails waving, awaiting the party's arrival. Simon was again faced with the gloomy prospects of being whipped to death. There was one slight ray of hope: perhaps his tormentors would want to save him for the stake in the big council house on ahead. There was no chance to dodge at Pickaway. Fortunately his experience in running the gantlet at Chillicothe kept him out of serious trouble. He escaped with only minor cuts and bruises. Simon could run faster and ward off the blows more effectively because he had approached Pickaway unbound and partly recovered from the abuse of the first days of his captivity.

Beyond Pickaway the trail led through a thick woodland. Trodding along this path Simon began philosophically to study his situation. Ahead of him at Wapotomika he would face a lingering, painful death at the stake. The time had arrived for him to try to escape. His muscular system had made a satisfactory adjustment during the long walk from Chillicothe, and he felt that with reasonable luck he could outrun his guardians. Escape now became a passion. The question of when and where to run was a haunting one. Every step he took brought him nearer the gantlet line which he knew was forming to greet his arrival at Machecheek.

Suddenly there was the roll of a drum and the terrifying yells of a band of natives. The Indians at Machecheek had become impatient for the sport and had run on ahead to Machecheek Mound to form twin lines. Simon was taken by surprise. Everywhere about him the Indians were wrought up. At the mound clubs and switches landed heavily. Simon was badly beaten, and he tripped and was knocked down. A snarling warrior smashed a handful of dirt into his face, stunning and blinding him.

The unexpected gantlet determined Simon to make a desperate break into the woods. This last run sapped most of the reserve strength he had built up in the last few days. When he was again headed down the trail, he was much less agile than he had been an hour before. What he lacked in physical strength, however, he made up in anger and determination to escape death. After he had traveled a short distance, he began to hear the monotonous beat of the drum. His torturers awaited the opportunity to administer a second beating for the day.

At Machecheek there was the familiar sight of the heartless gantlet. Again he saw the waving flails between him and the council house door. He was too exhausted even to attempt using strategy to run the line without being injured. He was going to take the quicker way out of his troubles. Behind him were the two warriors armed with knives waiting to give him a vigorous shove into the line. Near the council house door the drummer sat with his heavy club upraised ready to tap the starting signal. There was a breathless moment before the signal was given. For Simon this was his opportunity. He dashed forward in a flash and ran headlong for the woods. He ran the way he had run that night eight years before on the Kanawha when his camp was attacked.

Every long step Simon took he knew that he was running away from long nights of being stretched on the ground with every cell in his body aching. He was running from cruel Mazeppa rides on unbroken horses, from endless gantlets before the villages. He was diving headlong into the woods to avoid sooty posts and leaping flames in the council house at Wapotomika. Simon was living up to his old boast that given a decent chance he could outrun any Indian.

Kenton's fears for the moment were only of the Indians behind him. One thing mattered most and that was to reach the woods. He failed to watch out ahead and pitched into the midst of a mounted party of braves. The leader, Blue Jacket, rushed forward and took him prisoner. A heavy blow from the Indian's tomahawk upon his head dropped him in his tracks. He sank to the ground badly injured and unconscious. The Indians were more furious than ever. They threw him across a small stream in the mud and used his body for a bridge. When the last warrior had crossed over, and they removed him from the mire, he was almost dead.

Simon was ready to give up. He felt that even Providence had forsaken him. Already he had endured enough punishment to drive a man insane. His captors gave him a short breathing spell while they waited for their companions to come in from the trails. Eight miles away was Wapotomika—a name that had come to mean eternal doom for Simon. Simon was driven forward under heavy guard from Machecheek to Wapotomika. Already the village and the great council house were crowded with hundreds of Indians who had come long distances to dance themselves into a state of exhaustion around the fire of death.

Another gantlet awaited Kenton. Injured and weary, he was now less able to make any effort to protect himself. Again there were the savage clubs and the maddening drum. The loud yells had become a monotonous part of the horrible nightmare he had suffered during the last long days and nights. In his final race Simon was almost killed. The Indians knocked him down and then milled about him in a wild, screaming mob. But even in this mad storm he was saved. Flashing tomahawks and clubs only threatened, they did not rob the council house of its victim.

Simon was more dead than alive. Back at the creek where

the sharp heels of the warriors had buried his head in the mud, he had given up. There was little horror for him when he was tied to a stake in the council house, where he could watch the awkward procedures. In his misery Simon waited anxiously for the final stroke that would take his life.

CHAPTER 18

On The Road To Sandusky

Just as the gloom had settled down heaviest upon Simon, there was a nervous stir in the hall. The door opened and in walked Simon Girty with his brother James, John Woods, and a warrior. They came to bring the good news that they had captured eight prisoners in the white settlements along the upper Ohio. Among these were Mrs. Kennedy and seven children. The war party had also taken seven scalps. This required immediate consideration by the council. Simon was untied and led from the hall. There would be time later for the discussion of his case.

Girty's arrival was a godsend. Perhaps as Simon was led from the council house, he had a faint hope that his old friend of Dunmore's War would come to his aid. He recalled their solemn pledge of friendship.

Only Simon Girty could help him, but he had shown no signs of recognizing the prisoner. Kenton remembered the last time he had seen the unhappy "white Indian." It was in Pittsburgh when he had gone to meet George Rogers Clark. Girty was then a sad, disillusioned boy who expressed an intense hatred for the American backwoodsmen. He had expected to be a captain, but the frontier militiamen had ignored his requests.

They were in too much of a hurry to get home to worry with a boy. When the Revolutionary War began, he became an Indian agent of the British posts along the Great Lakes and was now helping in the efforts to destroy the Kentucky settlements.

When the question of the prisoners was settled, Simon Kenton was ordered back to the stake in the council house. Girty threw a blanket on the ground and commanded Kenton to be seated. Simon was stubborn. His independent Irish nature rebelled at the gruff command, and he stood rigid. Girty caught him by the sleeve and jerked him to the ground.

Once seated beside Girty, Simon learned that he was first to be questioned about Kentucky. Remembering Boone's command on that morning before Boonesborough when the fighting was hot, "to sell your lives as dearly as possible," he prepared to evade the questions.

"How many men are there in Kentucky?" asked Girty.

Simon replied, "It is impossible for me to answer that question, but I can tell you the number of officers and their respective ranks; you can then judge for yourself."

Girty then asked, "Do you know William Stewart?"

"Perfectly well," said Simon, "he is an old and intimate acquaintance."

Then came the dramatic moment. Girty asked Simon his name. In a clear ringing tone, Kenton replied, "Simon Butler." The enunication of his name came like a shot.

For the first time Simon Girty looked at the prisoner. He wished to see if he spoke the truth. He threw his arms around Simon's neck and greeted him with emotion. "You are condemned to die," he told Simon, "but I will use every means in my power to save you." Here was a ray of hope.

Girty turned to the council and spoke in the Shawnee tongue. He used his keen knowledge of Indian psychology. He told the Indians that he and their prisoner had roamed the woods and slept together in the same bed. They had faced many hardships side by side. Kenton was his sworn brother. He then asked the Indians for his sake to let the prisoner go free. There were many other white men in Kentucky, but this one was his friend. "For three years," Simon Girty told the council, "I have been your brother." He had been true to them, and they knew they could trust him. The Shawnee was a great lover of oratory, and Girty made a powerful appeal. His eloquent speech softened the countenances of some of the frowning warriors.

Some of the chiefs agreed at once to release Simon, but many others objected. One strong-willed warrior almost swayed the voting against Kenton by taunting the council for acting like women. He said the council had changed its mind every hour. Simon was a bad man. He was a brazen horse thief. He had killed one Indian, had wounded another, and had snapped his gun at still another. The prisoner had committed too many crimes against their people to be set free.

The warrior's speech was a clear statement of the Indians' sense of justice. His comparison of the council to a fickle women was embarrassing. Before the speaker could be seated, Simon Girty was again on his feet. This was his first and only request of them. Long ago he had proved his friendship for the Indian and on many occasions had rendered loyal service to them. It was now their turn to favor him. In his final appeal he played heavily upon the Shawnees' sentimentality. The council voted to set Simon free as a ward of Girty.

For the first time in several days Simon was able to lie down and rest with his limbs free to move as he pleased. The soot was scrubbed from his blackened face, and Girty bought him new clothing from a British trader. An Indian woman adopted him as a son, and during the next few days she went through an agonizing ceremony of having his body rubbed raw in order to wash the white blood and spirit out of his system. She poured water over his body and repeated in singsong fashion the magic words which would remove all traces of the white man.

Living with Girty in his cabin was pleasant. Kenton was given a horse and a saddle, and he was permitted to ride where he pleased among the villages. During twenty days of freedom, Simon, like Boone at Chillicothe, almost became an Indian. He recovered from the brutal whippings that had befallen him. The deep scalp wound healed, and once again he was in good physical condition.

Among the warriors were many dissatisfied chiefs who still believed that Simon should be burned at the stake. They reasoned that many of their friends had traveled a long way to attend the celebration, and now they were cheated. Even though the Indians were fond of their adopted brother Girty, there was no reason to let him outtalk them. The Shawnee was an impulsive creature. One moment he was friendly, the next he was sullen and angry. Although free, Simon was conscious that his presence was liable to cause trouble at any moment.

As a free man riding along the trails with Girty, Simon had numerous opportunities to escape to Kentucky. He never made known the reason why he did not run away. Doubtless it was his undying loyalty for his friend that kept him from leaving. Certainly if he could have looked into the future, he would have run away rather than go on to new trials.

A war party failed in a raid against the whites in Kentucky and returned to Chillicothe in a bad frame of mind. Members of the returning party stirred their brothers into a wild fit of anger. In the neighborhood of Wheeling some of their braves had been killed and others wounded. They were now ready to punish any white man who crossed their path.

The return of the defeated warriors was an excellent excuse for reopening Simon's case before the council. Warriors from the distant villages demanded that he be burned. They sent a

messenger to Solomon's Town, where Girty had his cabin, to return the prisoner. This decision came with the suddenness of a stroke of lightning. Girty, Kenton, and an Indian named Redpole were walking through the woods when they heard a loud, quavering whoop. Not far away they saw an Indian give the distress signal. Girty knew that this messenger was coming to tell of a council meeting and that it meant trouble for Kenton. The messenger came up and instructed Girty to go at once to the council house and to take his prisoner with him. Then the messenger shook hands with Girty and Redpole but ignored Simon. This was an evil sign.

When Girty and Simon reached the council house, the Indians were in an uproar. They shook hands with Girty, but again Kenton was ignored. Simon felt certain now that his three weeks of freedom were only a short reprieve from an unhappy ending. His appearance inside the council house fired the Indians' tempers. They were now determined that he should be turned over for punishment.

Once again Simon Girty appealed to the council to spare his white friend. He went over the same points for granting him this one favor as a reward for his loyalty to them. But this time the faces before him remained unchanged. The ancient hatred of their long-knifed enemy was throughly aroused. They were feeling the sharp sting of defeat which their braves had just suffered across the Ohio.

In Kentucky the settlers were robbing them of their rightful hunting ground. They were murdering their braves and stealing their horses. This was no time to show mercy to a white man. No longer would they play the part of weaklings and change their minds. In angry guttural tones, sweating orators stirred the passions of their fellows. One after another denied Girty's plea with a demand for Kenton's life at the stake.

Simon Kenton was forced once again to stand by and see the war club pounded violently upon the ground as it passed from hand to hand. Before the club had gone around the circle, he knew that Girty had lost his cause. In a genuine spirit of defeat and sadness, Girty leaned over and told Simon he would have to die.

There was nothing else Girty could say in his defense, but he could make an appeal to the Indians to delay the execution until weeks later when the British paid their Indian allies the yearly tribute for their services. Likewise, he asked that Simon be transferred to Sandusky where there would be a bigger crowd to see him punished. The chief agreed to this request. The more Indians they could gather around the stake, the happier they would be.

Five warriors were given the task of taking Simon to Sandusky. They were to keep a close watch on him to make certain that he did not escape. For Simon this journey was the beginning of another trail of torture. A short distance from Solomon's Town, where he had spent the last three weeks so pleasantly, Girty passed on horseback. He rode by the prisoner without even greeting him. Simon was now alone and deserted.

Simon walked on ahead of his guards with a long leather strap fastened securely about his neck. The party hastened through the woods, and the pace in warm weather was exhausting. At Silver Creek a halt was made to get water. When Simon had finished drinking, he very innocently stepped across the little stream to await the beginning of the journey. This move antagonized the Indians. They looked upon the act as one of impudence, and one of the warriors in a fit of hot temper hit the defenseless Simon with a tomahawk and broke his arm. The guards were in a hostile frame of mind. Back at Wapotomika they had won their argument in the face of bitter opposition. They were angry because they had been delayed so long in burning their prisoner. Simon was forced to go on despite the severe pain in his injured arm. If he had wavered or stopped, it would perhaps have meant death. Simon was marched through Solomon's Town, but there was no sign of Simon Girty. His sworn friend of Dunmore's War had at last turned against him.

Beyond the town Simon was again attacked, this time by a warrior with a heavy tomahawk. As the party made its way along the trail, they came upon an Indian woman chopping down a tree. Nearby sat her brave smoking his pipe. When the resting warrior saw the Indians with a white prisoner, he snatched the ax from the woman's hand and attacked Simon. The enraged Indian swung the ax at the prisoner's head, but Simon was able to dodge the fatal blow. In dodging, however, the ax landed on his collarbone and broke it. Simon was now almost too badly injured to walk. His arm and shoulder were so damaged that he lost the use of one side. If it had not been for the protection of his captors, he would have been chopped to pieces. In a discouraging vein of irony, they explained to the murderous warrior that Simon was an important prisoner on his way to suffer a public death.

The process of death had already begun. The tomahawk blows had killed Simon's spirit. There was one hope left. On the road to Sandusky, Simon learned, the party would pass near Chief Logan's cabin, and he remembered how sad Logan had been when he visited with him at the meeting of the treaty council. Late in the afternoon Simon and his captors arrived at the chief's lodge. Kenton's heart sank. Would John Logan know him or not? Already Simon Girty had deserted him, and he could scarcely hope for aid from the embittered Indian.

When the party stopped before the cabin, Logan came out to greet them. He addressed Simon in the scolding manner of a grandfather, "Well, young man, these young men seem very mad at you. But don't be disheartened, I am a great chief; you are to go to Sandusky; they speak of burning you there; but I will send two runners tomorrow to speak good for you."

Once inside the lodge, John Logan took charge of the crippled prisoner. He set Simon's broken bones and fastened them with clumsy splints. When at last Simon was comfortable, he and Logan talked of their hunting experiences in western Virginia. Chief Logan's old bitterness was gone. His manner was gentle, and before morning Simon began to hope that perhaps he would be spared the ordeal ahead of him.

By subtle persuasion Logan got Simon's guardians to stay over for a day's hunting with him. This was a precious day in Simon's life. It gave Logan an opportunity to arrange for his eventual release, and Simon had a chance to rest for a day before going on to the end of his journey.

Chief Logan's actions were mysterious. Simon began to wonder what, if anything, was being done on his behalf. He knew that Logan's runners had gone on a mission. Later that day they returned and went into secret council. But Simon remained ignorant of their news. The Indian liked the element of surprise. He found great pleasure in being vague in certain of his statements. Whenever it was possible, he expressed his sentiments in acts rather than in words. Chief Logan did not tell Simon what to expect at the end of his heartbreaking journey. He gave him bread and meat but left him to journey on in uncertainty. As Simon's hostile guardians once again drove him before them at the end of the long leather strap, he was sure that both his friends had failed him. They had been kind, but apparently neither had enough influence to save him. Simon was certain that this time he was going to die.

CHAPTER 19

Detroit Prisoner

Along the trail northward to Sandusky, Indians galloped out to see the famous prisoner, while the woods rang with quavering yells of triumph. Occasionally large companies of Indians were drawn up by the roadside to watch Simon pass. This was a bad sign. From his experience at the other villages, he foresaw that his entry to Sandusky would be a bitter trial. Nursing his crippled and feverish arm, he visualized a dozen times the long gantlet which he knew was waiting for him. But at Sandusky came momentary relief when he saw there was no anxious line waiting with upraised clubs and knives. Simon's sacrifice was to be an important one, and the chiefs were not taking any chances of having him knocked down and killed in a gantlet line.

When he reached the village common, he saw that he was to be burned. A strong stake was in place. From its top on a leather strap swung a horn of water for Simon to drink when the flames leaped up around him. A pile of dry wood awaited the torch. Already in his mind's eye Simon could see the Indians dancing around his writhing body, their wild screams growing louder as the fire burned brighter. When his pains became unbearable, the drums would be beaten in the loud monotonous roll of death. Other Kentuckians had gone to a similar fate, and Simon knew there was nothing left for him but to go to his end with as much bravery as possible.

The next morning dawned fair. It was a perfect fall day, a day especially designed for an Indian celebration. Simon was led out at sunrise and fastened to the stake. A slow fire was started in the pile of wood and slowly burned its way into the heavy pieces. Terrifying puffs of smoke rolled upward and strangled Simon. Long, jagged tongues of flames reached out at his clothes. In a few moments they would catch the fringes of his tattered breeches, and there would be the unbearable sting of the fire. He would suck at the horn of water in a frantic effort to stay his torture, then sag in the leather thongs in a state of unconsciousness. For Simon this would be the end.

Within the twinkling of an eye occured one of those strange freaks of nature so common in the Ohio Valley. A small, vaporous cloud swirled and drifted low overhead, and a sudden downpour of rain came to drench the flames at Simon's feet. His tormentors were frightened. Could this unexpected cloudburst be a sign that the gods were angry? Even so, the Indians were unwilling to free their prisoner. Perhaps the rain was merely a tempermental fit on the part of the Great Spirit, which within a short time would pass away.

But the delay caused by the rainstorm was the necessary interruption needed to bring Simon relief. While the Indians milled around the village waiting for both the great fire dance and the distribution of British goods, Peter Druillard arrived. Druillard, or Drewyer, as Simon called him, was a fantastic French Canadian. He was sent to the Indians with goods which he distributed among them as pay for their services in the war against the Americans. Druillard's arrival was an exciting event. For days the warriors had waited for him.

Druillard's long experience as a trader among the Indians

had taught him many lessons in primitive psychology. He had dressed himself in the colorful uniform of an English captain, and he was decorated with a grand display of jangling medals. He was an impressive sight to the excited warriors who huddled about him. But Druillard's influence was even greater than that of his gaudy uniform. It was he who controlled the gifts to the Indians. He could make rich gifts to the braves or, if they displeased him, he could withhold their presents. Druillard had received messages from both Girty and Logan to use his influence to secure Simon's freedom.

When the council assembled, Druillard asked for permission to address it. He said he did not like the American backwoodsmen, because they had caused the unhappy war. He hoped the day would come when the last one would be destroyed. Until then, however, the British and Indians would have to be cunning and take advantage of every opportunity to strike a heavy blow at them. Soon the time would come when they could cross the river into the Indian's territory just as they had crossed the mountains into Kentucky. The prisoner before him was an American. On many occasions he had scouted for frontier war parties and could tell them much of the settlements in Kentucky. At Detroit the British officers would want to ask him many questions about the Americans so as to know better how to meet the enemy.

This speech was a good beginning. It made sense to the council, but there was still the practical question of all the trouble Simon had caused them, and Druillard knew that he would have to forestall this objection if he was to save Simon. The prisoner, he said, had stolen horses, but the horses had been recovered. He had killed one of their braves on a former raid, and he snapped his gun at another, but they had Montgomery's scalp as part compensation for their loss. Kenton had already been punished before the villages in the long gantlets. He had been bound to the wild pony, and they had stretched him out on the ground night after night. This had taught Simon a lesson. They had gone to a lot of trouble to capture the prisoner and to bring him to Sandusky. He, Druillard, would pay them one hundred dollars for their trouble. Druillard then made a vague promise that perhaps the British would give the Indians some more money. They could reclaim the prisoner when the British were through with him.

Druillard's shrewd argument won. He paid the hundred dollars, and Simon was turned over to the British as a prisoner of war. Logan and Girty had saved him at last through the clever trader. As Druillard and one of the chiefs went toward Lower Sandusky with Simon, the captain began asking questions. He wanted to know something of the strength of Fort McIntosh. Likewise, he wished to know the strength of the forts in Kentucky. Simon avoided answering Druillard's questions. Frankly, he knew nothing about Fort McIntosh, and since he was only a private soldier and a woodsman, he pleaded that he knew little about the military strength of Kentucky.

As a British prisoner Simon was free from the tortures of the gantlet and the prospect of being burned at the stake. Even though in Kentucky the English governor at Detroit was called the "ha'r buyer," Simon knew that he would not be given back to the Indians. All along the way he was treated with kindness.

Kenton's broken bones healed quickly, although the arm was crooked because it had been improperly set. Rest and good food restored his strength. The party went overland to Lower Sandusky and then by boat to Detroit. Once again Simon was in robust health. The time he had spent as a prisoner of the Indians had almost drained the last ounce of his physical resistance. But his vigorous early years in the woods had toughened him, and his strong body was able to take a lot of cruel punishment. After the terrible experiences were ended, he looked back with some pride upon the fact that he was one of the few men in all history who had lived through a Mazeppa ride.

At Detroit the commanding officer spent some time questioning Simon about Kentucky. Like Druillard, he wished to know something of General McIntosh and his fort. Again Simon refused to give direct answers. The English officer treated him like a gentleman when he refused to divulge useful information.

Simon was not to be subjected to any harsh punishment as a prisoner of war. There were few restrictions placed upon him. He was instructed to report each morning to an officer and to stay within certain well-defined limits. Otherwise he was a free man. Dr. McGregor reset his arm and gave him good care. For Simon his imprisonment in Detroit was a fine excuse for spending the hard winter in comfortable quarters.

After Simon had become acquainted with the officials at Detroit, he quickly cultivated the friendship of the doctor, the storekeeper, John Edgar, and all the traders who drifted in from time to time. They all talked of the country and gave him much information about the woods and the location of Indian villages. In a sense he was standing behind the scenes watching the British part of the war in the Northwest. He was in Detroit at the time George Rogers Clark was capturing Hamilton's army at Vincennes.

In early spring the Indians brought several Kentucky prisoners to Detroit. Among them were Captain Nathan Bullitt and Jesse Coffer, both of whom Simon knew. Here was a possibility of escape. Simon now had trustworthy companions who would cooperate with him in an attempt to get back to Kentucky.

As the brisk northern spring days went by, Simon spent long hours chatting with his friends about Detroit. On clear mornings, with Coffer and Bullitt, he sprawled on a sunny spot of ground and planned their escape. Simon was determined to run away and go home. One thing stood in his way, however.

He had no gun, and it would almost be suicide to begin the journey unarmed.

Other matters also occupied Simon's attention. If the three Kentuckians were to make a successful escape, they would have to plan it carefully. Success would depend upon removing all suspicion beforehand. To do this, their irregular movements had to be made a matter of course. They made it a practice to go and come at all hours of the day, and occasionally they strayed to the limits of their bounds.

Hour after hour Simon sat by the stove in John Edgar's store and listened to gossip of the woods. The storekeeper and his wife grew fond of the good-natured Kentucky boy. To them he had become a sort of adopted son. When traders and Indians drifted in from the trails, Simon was on hand to talk with them. From all of them he pumped information. He was building a mental map of the region. Simon's eagerness for information at times revealed his intentions. A sly old Scotch trader named McKinzie told him that "if I was going to Kentucky I would go by way of the Wabash country, and not by the Indian villages."

Traders who had been friendly would, Simon knew, secure him a gun, but he needed the good will of the English officers. Everyone was good to Simon. He had a lot of information, but there was still the troubling question of the guns. Someone at Detroit would have to aid them, but who would do it? Simon asked himself this question over and over. Dr. McGregor had been kind, but he was a loyal Englishman, and John Edgar's future welfare depended upon his loyalty.

Perhaps Mrs. Edgar would help him; at least he would ask her. She received Simon's request with silence. In fact Simon was not certain that she knew what he meant. He had not come right out and asked for the guns. Simon knew the art of subtle approach, and he had suggested that the foliage was heavy and the trails were dry. It would be a fine thing for men who loved the woods to have guns at such a pleasant time of year.

Mrs. Edgar gave no hint of her reactions, and Simon wondered if she would fail him. The answer came suddenly a few days later, when he and the storekeeper were alone. John Edgar brought down from his storeroom an armload of moccasins and told Simon to pick out what he needed. Then Simon guessed that Mrs. Edgar would help him get guns! Not since Peter Druillard had led him away from the smoldering heap of wood at Sandusky had he been so happy. Soon he and Coffer and Bullitt would slip out the back way to the great swamp and begin their journey back to Kentucky.

Indians came to Detroit to sell their furs and to celebrate. When they stacked their guns in the open courtyard, the Kentuckians stole two of them, and Mrs. Edgar provided a third. In the garden back of the Edgar house, the prisoners found a store of supplies.

Under cover of darkness one warm June night, the three silent figures faded into the dark fringe of the woods. Simon's muscles were tense. His breath was drawn in long silent drafts. His feet located sure footing. It was important to get away as silently as possible.

For several days the escaping prisoners did not fire guns. During the day they remained in hiding, and under cover of darkness they hurried southward. It was a long journey from Detroit down the Wabash River and across the southern Indiana swamp to the Falls of the Ohio. Stretches of the route passed over marshy ground, and other parts led through unbroken forest. The going was rough. Fallen branches and sharp roots cut gashes in the soft moccasins. Briers and thorns tore at bare feet.

Every step that Simon took after the first two days of travel was painful, but more disturbing was the knowledge of their danger. When the going became tough, Simon's companions grumbled. They were hungry; their bodies were tired and stiff. Coffer and Bullitt wished to hurry on to Kentucky, but neither of them had ever been stretched out nor had they ever run a gantlet. Once Simon, too, had been careless, but now he was determined to avoid another siege of punishment. Hunger and despondency were nothing to him in the face of such agony.

One day the fugitives found themselves dangerously near an Indian encampment. Bullitt and Coffer became unnerved at the knowledge that the Indians were so close, and they talked of giving themselves up, but Simon's courage was high. Carefully he led his companions around the camp. When they were again buried in the woods, Simon shot a deer and the warm fresh meat raised the spirits of his companions. With a fresh supply of food they plunged on southward.

For thirty-three days Simon and the two Kentuckians made their way across the strange western woods. It was July when they at last crossed the Ohio River to Clark's settlement on Corn Island. Their bare feet were slashed and festered. Their clothes hung on their bodies in tatters. Their powder bags were empty, and they were starving. The journey had been a nightmare, but Simon was happy. He was home again. Kentucky needed his aid, and he was ready to help defend her. He had come back from the roughest adventure any Kentucky pioneer had ever experienced, and he had brought back with him much useful knowledge of Kentucky's enemies.

CHAPTER 20

Chillicothe Scout

For the moment the Indians were quiet. That old Kentucky blunderer, John Bowman, had been chased back across the river from an unsuccessful raid. Boonesborough was enjoying a spell of inactivity while the settlers built new homes and opened new fields around the fort. At Corn Island Colonel Clark's settlers were waiting for him to make his next move. He was still away at Vincennes. Perhaps he was planning a new campaign, but no one at Corn Island could tell Simon what was going to happen.

In a way it was disappointing for Simon to come home to Kentucky and find the people enjoying peace. Indian fighting had become a vital part of his existence. His chief interest in life was wrapped up in scouting the woods in search of an enemy. A few days at Corn Island gave him enough of civilization; a peaceful fortress was no place for a crack woodsman. If Clark intended to march against Detroit, then he needed Simon's aid.

Shouldering his rifle, Simon went off again to wade through the woods beyond the Ohio. His feet were scarcely healed from the grueling journey down from Detroit. But he was determined to go to Vincennes to see Clark and learn his plans. When Simon

arrived at Clark's headquarters, however, he found the chief of Long Knives in a state of indecision. From the very beginning, the plucky Virginian had secretly aimed his drive in the Northwest at the key British post of Detroit. Now there was serious doubt in his mind that it would be wise to continue the campaign.

Simon reported the conditions of the British force at Detroit as he had seen it. But already Clark had dealt the enemy two hard blows. To attempt a third one with so small an army and with limited supplies would be folly. Clark was not going on to Detroit. The northern campaign involved too much danger. One false step and he would lose everything he had gained.

Turning back to Kentucky, Simon spent the winter at Harrod's and at the new Fort Lexington. Every day people were coming over the trails and down the river with pack horses loaded with household goods. New settlements were springing up. Where Hinkston's blockhouse had stood, there was now

Ruddle's Station. Lexington had been founded, and five miles away the four Bryan brothers had located their settlement. All over the beautifully rolling limestone country, the Kentucky pioneers were making tomahawk notches on trees to mark their claims to the land. Simon's virgin Kentucky was in a state of rapid change.

Along the trails of the Licking country that fall, Simon saw squirrels putting away great stores of acorns and nuts. Birds were flying nervously through the woods toward the south. Long-necked, and squawking ganders and drakes led their wobbling V's of geese and ducks toward warmer weather. By the first week in November 1779, the woods were wrapped in a heavy coating of snow. Cold, blowing rains fell, and the water froze into a tight, glazed blanket of ice. Week after week of freezing weather went by. Food grew scarce at the forts. Simon went into the woods in search of game, but he found it starving. Rabbits could scarcely move about on their frostbitten feet, and their bodies were too poor for food. Buffalo, deer, and elk were either dead or so weakened from lack of food and the intense cold that they literally could not move out of his path. The skin of bears clung to their sharp backbones like limp cloth thrown over a thin ridgepole. At the forts both people and livestock sickened and died. This became known as Kentucky's "terrible winter."

When spring finally came, and the ice-covered trees thawed, there were again Indian signs on the Kentucky side of the Ohio River. First the warriors came in small scouting parties, and Simon discovered their presence along the upper Licking River trails. For a brief period he and a few companions tried to erect a station near where he and Williams had built their cabin, but the raiders forced them to give up and move back to the lower settlements.

Across the Ohio the British were again encouraging the

Indians to make a heavy drive against the Kentuckians. They wished to follow close on the heels of the hard winter and to strike a fatal blow at the white settlers. Colonel Byrd led this army of picked British and Indians. The Indian troops were given new guns, and a special company of warriors was supplied with brass cannon. Always before the Indians had met defeat at the fortress walls. But this time Colonel Byrd intended to knock down the fortifications and drive the white man out of the Kentucky country.

This well equipped army followed the Licking trails southward. It was going to take the stations as they came. At Ruddle's settlement, Byrd surprised and captured the station and robbed the houses. Indian warriors fought among themselves for the loot, and in a short time they were loaded down. To their way of thinking, wars were fought for plunder. Now that they had all the household goods they could carry, there was no use in attacking the other settlements. They refused to go on, and Colonel Byrd was forced to give up and return beyond the river.

Simon Kenton was at Harrod's Fort when he heard the news of the attack on Ruddle's. News of its capture brought back to him the spirit of the terrible year of the "three sevens." He set out at once with Charles Gatiffs to follow Byrd's army. Before the British and Indians had gone far, Simon and Gatiffs were close on their heels. At night, so it is said, while the Indians and British slept, the two rolled away one of their brass cannon.

When the invaders were safe across the Ohio, the border scouts rushed back to Harrod's to report the news. A messenger was sent at once to the Falls of the Ohio and then on to Vincennes to report the disaster at Ruddle's to George Rogers Clark. Harrod and the other Kentucky leaders hastened to organize their men. Clark sent orders that the Kentucky militiamen were to join him at the mouth of the Licking for a raid on the Indian villages beyond the river.

The drive was to start in August, and it would be directed at the villages of Chillicothe, Piqua, and Machecheek. When Clark's frontier army crossed the Ohio, Simon was proud captain of one company under Benjamin Logan's command. Years later a young Kentuckian recalled how he had seen Simon Kenton strutting along the trail at the head of his troops as a militia officer.

For Simon, the expedition against Chillicothe and Piqua was sweet revenge. On those hot August days he retraced some of his torturous route astride the bucking pony two years before. He came on the place where the Indians had treated him so cruelly in a night camp. In a short time the frontier army was at the place where the inhabitants of the village had danced wildly about his aching body. Clark had sent him ahead as master scout, and Simon led the whites up to the village limits to destroy it.

Colonel Clark's seasoned men had come well armed. They carried within their stalwart ranks twelve brass cannons to pay the Indians back in kind for their assault upon Kentucky. Their leader was an old hand at fighting a campaign a long way from his base of supplies and with limited stores. He rationed food and ammunition and organized the men into small, efficient fighting units.

When they attacked, Colonel Clark intended that his men should move forward according to a set plan. There was to be no wild shooting in which the whites strafed their own men. Infantrymen were to move quickly into positions where the line was weak. Artillery men were to take up well-covered posts and blast away at the cabins. Never before had an army of frontiersmen moved forward with better organization or with more destructive determination.

At Chillicothe, Colonel Clark did not have the advantage

of approaching his objective in strict secrecy as he had done at Kaskaskia and Vincennes. A traitorous white man ran ahead to announce the approach of the white army, so when the Kentuckians arrived before the village, they found it in ruins and the Indians in full retreat.

Piqua was not far away, and Clark moved on quickly to take the village by surprise. Before his men could cover the distance, however, a heavy rainstorm clogged the fuse holes of their rifles. Every man was ordered to fire his gun and then to reload in preparation for battle. This firing warned the Indians that the Kentuckians were in close pursuit.

The warriors came out to fight, but the frontiersmen were too powerful to be halted. Hardly had the fighting become hot before Simon Girty led his braves away from the battle, and soon most of the other Indians were in flight. Clark's cannons tore huge holes through flimsy cabins and wigwams. Sharpshooters hidden behind their walls were driven into the open and forced to run.

While the Indians fled headlong in defeat through the woods, flames leaped high among their cabins. Like Chillicothe, Piqua was burned to the ground, and Kentuckians used their tomahawks to destroy over five hundred acres of mature corn. They chopped down row after row of tall corn in payment for the hardships which the white settlers had faced for several years.

When the last row of cornstalks had been leveled and a good stock of the ears stripped off for food, a torch was applied to the field and the crop destroyed. Although Colonel Clark's men had failed to kill many Indians, they did ruin the villages. For the next two years the Indians were too busy finding food and building new villages to make a serious attack on Kentucky.

CHAPTER 21

Kentucky Is Free

Simon's caneland was very different now. It was a long time since he had stood atop the steep Ohio bluff late one spring afternoon and watched the wind sweep the tall cane into a vast wave of foliage. Everywhere Kentucky was changing. The buffalo no longer crossed the river in large herds to root about the salt licks. Elk were seldom seen any more, and other game was becoming scarce. Trails were rapidly being widened into roads, and cabins and fences were being built near every spring. Simon was no longer needed at the forts to supply food and scouting services. There were now unmolested fields which grew food, and the militiamen offered protection.

Keeping up with the changes taking place about him, Simon began a settlement on one of his land claims. It was not in the spot he would have chosen first of all, but the land was good, and it was close to the other settlements. The location was not far from Harrod's on a branch of Salt River. Stations were built by men who were industrious, by men who wanted to make good livings and to stay in one place for the rest of their lives. Simon had not changed his notions about work since he was sixteen. Hard work was for the other fellow; so, while his men

were busily engaged at building the cabins, he would slip away to the Licking country to chip more landmarks on trees.

Simon's business was fighting Indians and tramping through woods. Recently things had been too quiet, and he grew restless. The summer was hot. Tall corn in close rows grew near the forts. Years before, summertime had been the Indian raiding season, but now it seemed there would be no more raids.

Simon's fears that the sport of tracking down war parties was ended were needless. Beyond the Ohio the British officers were again stirring their native allies into making one more thrust at Kentucky. Under the leadership of white officers McKee, Caldwell, and Girty, the Indians were led across the Ohio to fall upon the unsuspecting Kentuckians. The British hoped to strike a death blow to the American settlements all along the whole frontier.

Caldwell led his army over practically the same route which Colonel Byrd had followed two years earlier. This time the

British and Indians were going to attack Bryan's Station. Their movement was quick and silent. They were going to strike while the men were away working in the cornfield and the women were washing at the spring. By one grand surprise rush, they hoped to capture the settlement and then go on to destroy the other stations.

Caldwell's strategy was brilliant, but he failed in its execution. The huge fort gates at Bryan's swung shut, and his army was too weak to force an entrance. On the fringe of the woods Simon Girty showed his face and taunted the besieged Kentuckians. Sticking their heads over the tall puncheon walls, the rowdy pioneers answered back with insults. They gave their dogs the name of Girty and shouted catcalls at him.

The raid against Bryan's had shown the invader's hand. No longer could he hope to win against the gathering militia force in Kentucky. George Rogers Clark was right; Kentucky had become too powerful for the British and Indians. After three days of waiting about the fort, Caldwell and his army turned back in retreat, and they followed the old buffalo trail northward to the river.

At the Licking River Daniel Boone halted the Kentucky militiamen. For a moment he stared toward the deep notch in the crest of the ridge beyond. Then he turned to Colonel John Todd and asked, "Colonel, do you see those two sneaking rascals standing there looking back? That's a mighty bad sign. They ain't a-scared one bit of us."

While Colonel Todd and the other officers watched, the two braves walked slowly from view.

Boone warned his companions, "It's a mighty bad time to attack. Those cowardly devils know they have the advantage."

Colonel Stephen Trigg pushed through the crowd to Boone's side. "What do you think we ought to do, Daniel?"

Again the woodsman ran his eyes along the top of the ridge,

and then replied, "Wait here, colonel, till Benjamin Logan and Simon Kenton come with their men. If there's an Indian left in Kentucky, Simon'll track him down for us."

Back in the crowd there was a commotion. Boone's advice displeased most of the men. Hugh McGary and other hotheads were moving toward the river. A moment later a horse splashed into the stream, there was a wild yell, and all the men rushed toward the other bank.

Unwilling to heed the warning of Daniel Boone, the mad frontiersmen charged up the hill at breakneck speed. They had lost their reason and were unwilling to wait for a scout to go ahead and locate Indians. No one in the party knew where the Indians were hiding nor at what moment they would strike.

Across the hill, the British and Indians heard the wild yell of their pursuers and quietly withdrew into the dense underbrush of a deep ravine. There they waited. Within a few minutes the Kentuckians were dashing over the hill and charging headlong toward the sheltered ravine. The loud roar of a rifle came from the underbrush, and a white horseman toppled from his mount. Then came a volley of shots in which most of the bullets found their marks. A moment later the ground was covered with wounded and dying men. Quickly a wild shout went up from the brush, and a stream of howling Indians poured out in hot pursuit of the retreating Kentuckians.

Off to one side Daniel Boone watched the progress of the battle. Not far away from where he stood, he saw his son stumble and then fall forward, dead. Daniel rushed in amidst the firing and rescued the boy's dead body and tucked it away under a fallen tree so that the Indians would not hack it to pieces.

The day after the battle Benjamin Logan and Simon Kenton arrived with their men. Saddened by the loss of his son, Daniel Boone shook his old friend Kenton's hand and said, "I wish you had been here yesterday. There never was a time in Kentucky when we needed a good Indian scout more." All around him, Simon saw men dishearted by the defeat at Blue Licks. "It was the worst thing that ever happened in the western country," said one of the men from Bryan's Station. Another looked up from his task of repairing a gun and said, "Our men fell just like weeds in front of a fresh-whetted scythe. At the first crack of the gun everybody in front was knocked down."

Beyond the long hill above the river Simon helped Logan's men gather the mangled bodies of the Kentuckians and place them in one large grave. Three of the officers had been quartered. As Simon helped bury the bodies of the fallen men, he recalled that seven years before near that same spot he had found the ashes and bones of Hendricks.

When George Rogers Clark got back to the Falls of the Ohio, news of the defeat at Blue Licks stirred his wrath anew. Again he organized the Kentuckians to cross the Ohio and destroy the Indian villages. Everywhere there was stir and bustle among the men on their way to meet Colonel Clark at the mouth of the Licking. Again Simon marched away as captain of a company, but at the Licking Clark made him chief scout. For the fourth time Simon tramped through the woods to Chillicothe. This time he was leading the Kentuckians up the Little Miami to strike a second destructive blow at the villages.

Five Indian villages were destroyed in this attack, but again their inhabitants fled before Clark's army. When the cabins and wigwams were aflame, the Kentuckians turned to the corn-fields. They left starvation and ruin in their path when they withdrew from the Ohio country. Simon's scouting had led the way to Clark's success.

When the Kentucky troops were back at the steep hills where Cincinnati now stands, Clark dismissed his men. But before he could order them to disband, a wave of sadness swept over them. Captain V. McCracken had received a mortal wound in the arm. Stretcher bearers eased his body down the steep river bluff, but before they reached the water's edge, he was dead. This young officer had stood shoulder to shoulder with Simon in the bitter fight at Chillicothe, and his death was a blow.

With his last words McCracken had asked his companions to hold a reunion of Clark's men on that spot fifty years later. Colonel Robert Floyd drafted resolutions, and the men shouted a lusty "Aye!" On November 4, 1832, those still alive would meet there in celebration of their victory against the Indians.

George Rogers Clark's army came back to Kentucky from Ohio to enjoy its victory. Once across the river, Clark assembled his remaining men to say good-bye to them. As the company broke into small knots, he turned to Kenton and said, "Well, Simon, this is the last of our big Indian raids. They have lost their English allies, and we have ruined their villages over the Ohio. The western country will grow fast now that the war is ended."

Simon knew that Clark had spoken wisely. There would be no more big raids that year. When he covered the Kentuckians' withdrawal from the Shawnee villages, they were in complete ruin. Already winter had arrived, and the braves could not get enough food to supply them on a long drive across the river. As Simon prepared to leave Clark's last camp at the mouth of the Licking, he knew the truth—Kentucky was free.

CHAPTER 22

Home To Virginia

L ife for Simon was beginning to take on new meaning. When he returned from Clark's campaigns, he was twenty-seven years of age, and once again he found himself living in a civilized community. He lived in a society where he would have to compete with his fellows for a living. Eleven years before he had escaped from such a fate, but the white man was moving across the frontier too fast even for Simon to keep ahead of the settlements.

Soon after Kenton came back from Detroit, he became interested in the new stream of settlers moving in from Virginia. Among the new arrivals were people who had lived in his old home county of Fauquier. For nine years he had heard nothing of his people, and during this whole time he was called Simon Butler. The name "Butler" had once meant freedom for Simon, but now it had come to be almost a badge of cowardice and disgrace.

The more Simon lived among the settlers, the more he began to think of his earlier life, to wonder if his people were still living. What had happened after he left? All this time he had been afraid the name "Kenton" would betray him.

As the years passed, Simon lost most of his old fear of being hanged. He began to hope that perhaps he had not killed William Leachman after all. It now seemed so ridiculous for him to have lost his head when he was in love with Ellen Cummins. Then one day there came freedom. From some mysterious source through the gossip of the frontier, the news came that William Leachman was alive. Years later people loved to tell many nice little stories of how Simon heard about Leachman. One was that his brother John had come out to Kentucky and recognized Simon. Others told how an old neighbor saw him and shouted, "Why, there's Mark Kenton's boy!"

With his own name again, Simon was an independent, happy man. The old Leachman trouble fell from his shoulders as if it had been a quarter of buffalo meat. Simon was proud to call himself "Kenton" again.

He was happy to hear that Mark and Mary Kenton were still alive. Their old home community had undergone many changes. Fauquier neighbors had grown poor with the land and moved on to make a new beginning on more fertile soil. Many of them had died along the trails to Lexington and Bryan's Station. Those who now lived neighbors to Simon in Kentucky spent hours telling him what had happened back in Virginia. Their long tales stirred up a homesickness he could not brush aside. He was determined to go back to Virginia to visit his people. Perhaps he would bring them out to Kentucky to live near him.

The clearings ate big holes into the forest around Simon's station, and as rude cabin walls climbed higher and higher above the ground, he became more sentimental about his earlier days. A return to civilization had set him to thinking of his people.

While Kenton's neighbors slaved at making new homes for themselves, he was making his own plans and looking toward the future. When he led the way as head chain bearer, or hacked claimmarks on trees, he became intoxicated with these dreams.

He was caught up in the desire of the American frontiersman to build for himself and his people a home of safety and plenty.

Like many another American son of poor parents, he hoped at last to lighten the labors of his aged father and mother. One crop from the rich Kentucky lands would equal a half dozen from those exhausted patches which each year sapped Mark Kenton's strength.

Spring and summer saw a big change take place among the Quick's Run cabins. Their shiny new split-board roofs bristled in the hot sun like sheets of gold. Flowers bloomed near the doorways in bright patches of color. Happy voices of singing women and girls rang out above the whirring of wheels and looms. Hens cackled about their nests, and not far away impatient calves bleated for their mothers grazing in the woods. Waving stalks of corn in thick rows crowded up to the yards just as the woods had done a year before. There was a sense of peace and security in this scene. Even the long rifles resting on the buckhorns above the doors had not been down for months. Kentucky was a land of white homelovers.

No one was aware of Simon's departure. He had always come and gone as he pleased. But this time Simon was going on the long journey home, retracing his steps of years before. He followed the Ohio River northward to Pittsburgh, and then went across the mountains to Mark Kenton's cabin.

When Simon came to the top of Bull Run Mountain, he paused a moment and gazed down at his old home. There were changes all about him. The woods had been cut away. Red splotches of poor, exhausted soil showed through the pitiful thin stalks of withered corn. The log cabin looked natural except, like the man who built it, it was old and worn. Rain and sun had bleached its logs and boards an ugly gray; its windows sagged like ancient eyelids. The yard about it was washed bare except where drooping clumps of Mary Kenton's flowers were starved for water. Gullies here and there cut their ugly traces across the scene before him. But there it was—Mark Kenton's cabin!

Simon wondered if his people would know him. Would they recognize their seventh child? Would his mother know the baby whom she had nursed while the British fought the French and Indians? He plunged down the hill. Mark met him at the door. For a minute the old man stared at the boy and then asked eagerly, "Ain't you Simon?"

Simon shook his father's hand and said, "Hit's been many a day since I was here."

Mark was excited at seeing his son again and began shouting for Mary to come at once from the garden where she was working.

Simon was over six feet tall and weighed a hundred and ninety pounds. A roll of auburn hair showed beneath his cap. The gangling boy of sixteen had grown into a handsome man.

"You're such a man now, and hit don't seem no time since I was holding you in my lap. Many's the nights I have wondered what had become of you. I used to dream about you. When you went away we tried to find a trace of you, but no one could help us," Mary told Simon.

It was a joyous homecoming. Old Mark was happy. There were tears in Mary's eyes as she held her son's hand.

There were dozens of questions Simon wanted to ask his father and mother. He was anxious to hear the story of his family. Where were his brothers? Where were his sisters? Where were the neighbors who had not moved away to Kentucky?

Young Mark had served in the army under George Washington. William now had six children. All of Simon's sisters were married, and even the least one had children. Frances and Benjamin were dead.

"What's happened to William Leachman?" Simon asked in a half-embarrassed manner.

"Why, he's a mighty sad man, son," replied Mark. "Life's been tough on him. Ellen died a year or two ago, and Bill's tryin' hard to raise their children." Then old Mark recalled how Leachman's father had found him on the day Simon ran away. "His pappy got worried when William didn't come back, and he went to see what had happened. Near the stump of the board tree, he saw William lying with his hair tangled in the bush. William was unconscious and he was beat into a pulp, but in a few days he was all right. He's forgiven you, and he will be happy to know you have come home."

William Leachman was among the old neighbors who came in the evenings to visit with Simon. The two shook hands and forgot their old quarrel. Simon was bubbling over with hair-raising stories. Night after night he sat on the porch and related his experiences among the Indians. His neighbors leaned forward, scrubby chins resting on calloused hands, to catch every word. Simon's return was an important event in their drab lives.

They wanted firsthand information that was vital to them. For the last seven or eight years stories of the fine Kentucky land had drifted back. It was a place, they had heard, where a man could get ahead in the world. They asked Simon dozens of questions about this new country. They had grown old and tired working the barren soil of their homes; they wanted to move on.

Simon sat there and listened to the eager questions. He knew what these anxious neighbors had in mind. He had, he told them, land enough for everybody. His generous Irish nature got the better of him there among his poverty-ridden friends. He was an excellent promoter of the Kentucky frontier, and he encouraged them to move away to the West.

Simon prepared to move his own family to the frontier. Mark was feeble, but his children packed up his household things for him. They pulled up his roots from the place where he had raised his family. They took him away from the poor land and the crude cabin he had built with his own hands. Setting forth on wobbly legs, Mark Kenton began a new adventure at an age when most men wanted to be in the stillness of their shady porches.

Nearly all of Mark Kenton's family set forth on the trail to Kentucky. They traveled slowly over the old road to Redstone. Pack horses were heavily loaded with household goods. Huge baskets of chickens, geese, guineas, and ducks rocked back and forth on other horses. Ahead of the procession the men and boys drove cattle and hogs. Simon, like Joseph, was leading his people to a happier land.

At Redstone on the Monongahela River the party halted to build a long, awkward Kentucky flatboat. Simon led the way to the woods to cut and hew the log beams for the boat. Three of the men sliced thick planks from logs with a whipsaw for the bottoms and sides.

On every hand was feverish activity. But Mark was exhausted. The long pull up the hills to the river had been too much for him. While his family was busy about the camp, he became seriously ill. His home had always been east of the mountains, and it was soon apparent that he was not to leave that land.

There by his side of the Monongahela, in the very doorway of the American frontier, Mark's sons lowered his wrinkled old body into a deep grave dug in the clay. There was no marker to say who was buried there.

Slowly the Kentons drifted southward to the Falls of the Ohio. Simon was impatient, and he and one of his brothers left the boat at Limestone and rode across the country. From the Falls of the Ohio the long train of family pack horses and livestock found its way to Quick's Run.

The Salt River valley, however, did not hold the fascination for Simon as did that along the Licking. He was anxious to get back to the Limestone country beyond the Kentucky. He wanted to go back where he would be close to the Ohio. He would build a strong blockhouse and give aid to hundreds of newcomers who drifted southward. And he would be close enough to the Ohio country to enjoy the sport of an occasional Indian raid.

Simon spent much of the winter of 1784 and 1785 surveying land above the Licking. He began to construct his station on land which he and Williams had first claimed. Before it was finished, an Indian party crossed the river and killed several settlers. Again Simon was forced to give up living near the Ohio and move back to the safety of the lower settlements.

After the attacks upon the settlers at Limestone, Simon knew better than ever that there should be a northern settlement. He returned to build one. He erected a strong blockhouse and gathered his relatives around him. Immigrants coming down the river were persuaded to settle close by. Thus it was that Simon became the guiding spirit in northern Kentucky. Rapidly he converted his hunter's dreamland into a white man's prosperous settlement. Kenton's name will live long along the Ohio in the county named for him. The hills of the Licking River country have been stripped bare of timber, but the spirit of the genial woodsman and pioneer still lingers there.

BIBLIOGRAPHY

The American Pioneer. 2 vols. Cincinnati, 1842-1843.

Bakeless, John. *Daniel Boone, Master Of The Wilderness.* New York, 1939.

Boyd, Thomas Alexander. *Simon Girty, the White Savage.* New York, 1928.

Burnet, Jacob. *Notes on the Early Settlement of the North-Western Territory.* Cincinnati, 1847.

Butterfield, Consul Willshire. *History of the Girtys.* Cincinnati, 1890.

Clift, G. Glenn. *History of Maysville and Mason County.* Lexington, 1936.

Cochran, Samuel L. *Simon Kenton.* Strasburg, Va., 1932.

Collins, Lewis, and Richard H. *History of Kentucky.* 2 vols. Covington, 1874.

Connelley, William E., and E. M. Coulter. *History of Kentucky.* 5 vols. New York, 1922.

Cotterill, Robert S. *History of Pioneer Kentucky.* Cincinnati, 1917.

Crafts, William A. *Pioneers in the Settlement of America.* Boston 1877.

Doddridge, Joseph. *Notes on the Settlement and Indian Wars of Virginia and Pennsylvania from 1763 to 1783.* Albany, N.Y., 1873.

Ellett, Elizabeth Fries. *Pioneer Women of the West.* New York, 1856.

English, William H. *Conquest of the Country Northwest of the Ohio River.* Indianapolis, 1897.

Hartley, Cecil B. *Life and Adventures of Lewis Wetzel, the Virginia Ranger.* Philadelphia, 1860.

Howe, Henry. *Historical Collections of Ohio.* 2 vols. Cincinnati, 1908.

Isenburg, James L. *George Rogers Clark, Fort Harrod's Pioneer Hero of the American Revolution.* Harrodsburg, Ky., 1939.

Jefferson, Thomas. *Notes on Virginia.* Richmond, 1805.

Kenton, Edna. *Simon Kenton; His Life and Period, 1755-1836.* New York, 1930.

Lester, William Stewart. *The Transylvania Colony.* Spencer, Ind., 1936.

Mackoy, Harry Brent. *Simon Kenton as Soldier, Scout, and Citizen.* Lexington, 1936.

Magazine of American History, vol. XV.

McDonald, John. *Biographical Sketches of General Nathaniel Massie, General Duncan McArthur, Captain William Wells and General Simon Kenton.* Dayton, Ohio, 1852.

McClung, John A. *Sketches of Western Adventure.* Dayton, Ohio, 1827.

McFarland, R. W. "Simon Kenton," *Ohio Archaeological and Historical Society Publications,* vol. 13, pp. 1-39.

Ohio Archaeological and Historical Society Publications, vols. 1-14.

Person, William. *Pioneer Life in the West, Comprising the Adventures of Boone, Kenton, Brady, Clarke, the Whetzels, and others . . .* Philadelphia, 1858.

Ranck, George W. *Boonesborough.* Louisville, 1901.

_____. *The Story of Bryan's Station.* Lexington, 1896.

Roosevelt, Theodore. *The Winning of the West.* 5 vols. New York, 1905.

"Simon Kenton," *Harper's New Monthly Magazine,* 28 (February, 1864).

Skinner, Constance Lindsay. *Pioneers of the Old Southwest.* New Haven, 1921.

Smith, Z. F. *The History of Kentucky.* Louisville, 1886.

Stipp, G. W. *The Western Miscellany, or Accounts Historical, Biographical and Amusing.* Xenia, Ohio, 1827.

Thwaites, Reuben Gold. *Early Western Travels, 1748-1846,* vols. 1, 3, 26. Cleveland, 1907.

Wilson, Samuel M. *Battle of the Blue Licks, August 19, 1782.* Lexington, 1927.

Withers, Alexander Scott. *Chronicles of Border Warfare,* ed. by Reuben Gold Thwaites. Cincinnati, 1895.